D1566529

# CIRCULATING BEING

PERSPECTIVES IN CONTINENTAL PHILOSOPHY SERIES
John D. Caputo, series editor

1. John D. Caputo, ed., *Deconstruction in a Nutshell: A Conversation with Jacques Derrida*
2. Michael D. Barber, *Ethical Hermeneutics: Rationality in Enrique Düssel's Philosophy of Liberation*
3. Michael Strawser, *Both/And: Reading Kierkegaard—From Irony to Edification*
4. James H. Olthuis, ed., *Knowing Other-wise: Philosophy at the Threshold of Spirituality*
5. James C. Swindal, *Reflection Revisited: Jürgen Habermas's Discursive Theory of Truth*
6. Richard Kearney, *Poetics of Imagining: Modern and Postmodern,* second edition

# CIRCULATING BEING

## From Embodiment to Incorporation

### ESSAYS ON LATE EXISTENTIALISM

THOMAS W. BUSCH

Fordham University Press
New York
1999

Perspectives in Continental Philosophy, No. 7
ISSN 1089-3938


Library of Congress Cataloging-in-Publication Data

Busch, Thomas W., 1937–
    Circulating being : from embodiment to incorporation (essays on
late existentialism) / Thomas W. Busch. — 1st ed.
        p.   cm. — (Perspectives in continental philosophy ; no. 7)
    Includes bibliographical references and index.
    ISBN 0-8232-1928-3 (hc). — ISBN 0-8232-1929-1 (pbk.)
    1. Existentialism.   I. Title.   II. Series.
B819.B87    1999
142'.78—DC21                                                    99-31411
                                                                   CIP

99   00   01   02   03   5   4   3   2   1
Printed in the United States of America
First Edition

*For Caitlin, John, Jay, Ailey,*
*Cole, Cecily and Michael, Aidan*
*. . . and those to come*

# CONTENTS

# PREFACE

There is nothing to express, nothing with which to express, nothing from which to express, no power to express, no desire to express, together with the obligation to express.

—Samuel Beckett

It is tempting to think of existentialism as a brilliant flash of lightning across the philosophical sky, both intense and brief. An indelible impression and disappearance into the void. Once and done. What could be more "existential"? Professional catalogers and encyclopedists of thought encourage this attitude by seeking to precisely mark existentialism's birth and death. Existentialism, it is commonly held by these outliners of thought, is "pre" to today's "posts"—relegated, ironically, to share philosophical identity with those systems of thought it so forcefully criticized.

Early scholarship on existentialism established its reputation as a countercultural movement, a radical critique of rationalism, idealism, scientism, technocracy, and bureaucracy in the name of embodiment, perspectivism, lived experience, contingency, and individualism. In the 1960s attention abruptly shifted in Europe to structuralism, and thence to poststructuralism and postmodernism, to a type of thinking that stressed the impersonal—the system, the unconscious, grammar, text. The heralds of this new thinking eagerly sought to take their distance from their existentialist teachers. The situation can be summed up in a small episode that occurred in the midst of the 1968 events in Paris, when Sartre, who, more than any other living writer represented existentialism, wanted, at a large and enthusiastic gathering, to publicly express his support for students and workers. He was grudgingly "permitted" to speak by those in charge because his name was still useful. As he eagerly approached the podium he found a message: Sartre, be brief!

Existentialism both proclaimed human finitude and opened up the question of philosophy's fate once finitude had been fully acknowledged. Existentialism's own identity, however, appears fixed by the scholarship that first established its reputation as a philosophy of the lived experience of a highly individualistic subjectivity and then led to its rejection on those very grounds by poststructuralism and postmodernism. This obscures the fact that existentialism made possible in significant ways what occurs in present forms of Continental philosophy, all of which assume the existentialist critique of dualism, essentialism, and totality in modern philosophy, while at the same time, existentialism remains capable of haunting today's scene as an important and relevant critic. Fortunately, recent scholarship is helping to sort out the relationship between certain existentialist philosophers (for it is important to recognize their differences) and the contemporary scene, for example, *Nietzsche's French Legacy,* by Alan Schrift, *Kierkegaard in Post/Modernity,* edited by Martin Matustik and Merold Westphal, John Caputo's *Radical Hermeneutics* and *Demythologizing Heidegger,* and Thomas Flynn's *Sartre, Foucault, and Historical Reason.*[1] Existentialism's story is still being written.

The essays in this volume offer a modest contribution toward filling out the story. Many fine studies of Camus, Marcel, Sartre, and Merleau-Ponty have traced out and definitively established the centrality of embodiment and lived experience in their works. What is far less established and publicized is how their works, particularly their late works, move beyond, without denying, embodiment to what I call "incorporation," the transcendence of individual experience in the discursive circulation of Being, a circulation which, while admitting individual differences, calls discussants together ethically and politically. The traditional treatment of the questions of universality and particularity, identity and difference, are translated from the register of abstract metaphysical principles to that of the circulation of Being in art, ethics, and politics. While each of these thinkers reacts critically to rationalism and idealism by stressing embodiment and individual experience, their later works converge in intimations of a communicative rationality which is also a call to shared communicative life. Camus writes of the "mutual understanding and communication" implied in rebellion, Marcel of "fraternal comprehension" which is the vocation of thought, Sartre of "the appeal for freedom addressed to all other men" implied in literature, and Merleau-Ponty of the "response" called for by works of art as "accomplishment and brotherhood." Their convergence on communicative rationality and communicative life is extended to their agreement on art as exemplar of communication, marking their distinctive approach to the important issue of understanding the relationship between universality and particularity. It becomes clear that their early assertion of individualism and rejection of essences was not to result in a rejection of universality *tout court,* but in a radical rethinking of it. In fact, at least in the case of the thinkers represented here, existentialism turns out to be not at all a repudiation or destruction of the Western philosophical tradition, but a vigorous attempt to reconstruct it.

## NOTE

1. Alan Schrift, *Nietzsche's French Legacy: A Genealogy of Poststructuralism* (New York: Routledge, 1995); Martin Matustik and Merold Westphal, eds., *Kierkegaard and Post/Modernity* (New York: Fordham University Press, 1995); John D. Caputo, *Radical Hermeneutics: Repetition, Deconstruction, and the Hermeneutic Project* (Bloomington: Indiana University Press, 1987); *Demythologizing Heidegger* (Bloomington: Indiana University Press, 1993); Thomas R. Flynn, *Sartre, Foucault, and Historical Reason: Toward an Existentialist Theory of History* (Chicago: University of Chicago Press, 1997).

# ACKNOWLEDGMENTS

In this enterprise, as in all aspects of my life, I find myself indebted to a number of people who have supported me in many ways. Dr. John Johannes, Vice President for Academic Affairs, and Rev. Kail Ellis, O.S.A., Dean of the College of Arts and Sciences, Villanova University, were kind enough to award me sabbatical leave to complete the book. My colleague John Caputo has been a constant source of helpful philosophical dialogue and wise advice. Thomas Flynn offered a number of valuable suggestions as the manuscript was put into its final shape. David Sprintzen was generous in sharing his expertise on Albert Camus. Jonathan Lawrence was an enormously helpful copy editor. And, most of all, my gratitude is extended to my wife, Nancy, who is always there and an invaluable part of all I do.

Kluwer Academic Publishers, publishers of *Continental Philosophy Review* (formerly *Man and World*), have kindly permitted me to use material from my article "Ethics and Ontology: Levinas and Merleau-Ponty" (Fall 1995). Chapter 2 is a revision and expansion of my article "Secondary Reflection as Interpretation," which appeared in the *Bulletin de la Société Americaine de Philosophie de Langue Française* (Fall 1995). Chapter 5 employs material from my article "Perception, Finitude, and Transgression: A Note on Merleau-Ponty and Ricoeur," in *Merleau-Ponty, Hermeneutics, and Postmodernism,* edited by Thomas W. Busch and Shaun Gallagher (Albany: State University of New York Press, 1992), with permission of the publisher.

# CIRCULATING BEING

# 1

# Albert Camus: Absurdity, Solidarity, and Difference

ALBERT CAMUS WAS, without doubt, a writer in whom thought and feeling, or life experience, were inextricably intertwined. The hazard for such writers is that their thought may appear too dated because too closely referencing past and (now) irrelevant situations. Camus's work, however, seems yet to speak to people as it finds continuous reprintings. My undergraduate students over the years have been very warm to Camus, much admiring, they tell me, his critical honesty, his embrace of the concrete, especially the physical, his rebelliousness, his overall sense of decency. These are qualities that I also have always respected in Camus, but lately his philosophical writings have taken on a new relevance for me in the light of today's postmetaphysical sensibility—particularly, current efforts to develop a postmetaphysical ethics and politics. I believe it is possible to see in Camus's own wrestling with these issues a forecasting of much present-day thinking in this regard. In this context, I propose to examine three critical episodes in Camus's life and works. The first was his contraction of tuberculosis early in life, which led to his elaboration of the absurd and the taking up of a nonmetaphysical ground of thinking. The second was his participation in the Resistance movement, which sparked his enthusiasm for community and a sense of solidarity capable of overcoming differences. The third was the Algerian crisis, which provoked him to reconsider the relation between the universal and differences.

I

In January 1931, *Le Rua,* the weekly sports report of Racing Universitaire Algerois, the sports division of the Association Générale des Etudiants d'Algérie, noted that the young (soccer) goalkeeper Albert Camus had been absent from play because of illness.[1] Indeed, Camus had developed a persistent cough and had lately been vomiting blood. Taken to a hospital, he was diagnosed with tuberculosis of the right lung. Camus had just turned seventeen. For a thinker such as he, so deeply committed to life experience, this illness, which was to afflict him through the remaining twenty-nine years of his life, was pivotal. The experience of the young man's passion for life in a diseased body underwrites the views on absurdity and revolt he subsequently developed.

When in 1958 Camus, now a recent winner of the Nobel Prize for literature, wrote a preface for the republication of his first book, he claimed that "about life itself I know no more than what is said so clumsily in *The Wrong Side and the Right Side*" (LCE 13). The title of this deeply autobiographical work expresses the young author's inability to pull together his contrasting experiences of life, specifically, the brimming outgoing energy of a healthy body and the exhaustion, self-absorption, and withdrawal of the sickly body. The central player in the essays is the body, which represents the paradox of life itself in its glorious sensuality, to which Camus would yield gladly and unreservedly, and also in its limits, its breakdown in hunger, fatigue, disease, and death, which repel him. The young Camus is alternately tempted to both mysticism and despair, to an absolute yes or no. Yet, he insists: "I don't want to bring myself to choose between them." He commits himself to remain poised "between yes and no" (LCE 51, 39).

Reading these words philosophically, one could say that Camus is committing himself to the *doxa,* the realm of appearance, relativity, antinomy, the very stuff traditional Western philosophers and theologians have set about to straighten out, rationalize, and remove for us in order to relieve our existential perplexity, doubt, fear, and terror. This becomes evident in *The Myth of Sisyphus,* where Camus installs himself in philosophical discourse. His own temptation, in his early work, to repress limits for an unqualified yes is figured in the move of the traditional philosopher and theologian to transcend the *doxa* to a higher level where all apparent incoherence, contradictions, and aporias are solved. Behind this move, this temptation toward absolute affirmation of meaning, which Camus experienced in himself and sees reflected in tradi-tional Western metaphysics and theology, he sees a deep existen-tial demand or "nostalgia" for coherence: "The mind's deepest desire, even in its most elaborate operations, parallels man's un-conscious feeling in the face of his universe: it is an insistence upon familiarity" (MS 17). To be familiar (family) is to belong. If true knowledge were possible, so Camus argues, then the knower (human desire) and the known (reality) would belong together, would be a perfect match for one another. Reality would be co-herent. Thus, for Camus, our metaphysics, our great metanarra-tives, which guarantee that reality is meaningful, are a reflection of an existential insistence upon meaning: "That nostalgia for unity, that appetite for the absolute illustrates the essential impulse of the human drama. But the fact of that nostalgia's existence does not imply that it is to be . . . satisfied" (MS 17). In fact, Camus claims that there is no "true knowledge." He appears to include by this several well-known philosophical strategies. First of all, he is indeed suspicious of what François Lyotard calls metanarratives, grand unifying stories: "So long as the mind keeps silent in the motionless world of its hopes, everything is reflected and arranged in the unity of its nostalgia. But with its first move this world cracks and tumbles; an infinite number of shimmering fragments is offered to the understanding" (MS 18). The multiplicity and diversity of life experiences resist reduction to intelligible unity, with the result that absurdist consciousness, in true postmodern (Lyotardian) spirit, is led to acknowledge that "there is no truth, but merely truths. From the evening breeze to this hand on my shoulder, everything has its truth" (MS 43).

Husserl's phenomenology is appealing to the young nominalist only insofar as it is restricted to its descriptions, for "thinking is learning all over again to see, directing one's consciousness, mak-ing of every image a privileged place" (MS 43). While delighted to find in Husserl a shared "taste for the concrete," Camus is disappointed with Husserl's "intellectualism," which seeks "extra-temporal essences" that would sum up all that the factical offers. Once more the "guise of the great principle" shows itself in the move to an eidetic level of theorizing which would clarify the "successive and incoherent" stream of life in the form of ex-plicit, definable packages, rendering life into science. Speaking of science itself and its attempt to make the world "familiar" (the attempt "to assure me that this world is mine"), Camus asserts that when science delves beneath the realm of the sensible appearance it is constrained to employ productive imagination: "You explain this world to me with an image. I realize then that you have been reduced to poetry. I shall never know. Have I the time to become indignant? You have already changed theories. So that science that was to teach me everything ends up in a hypothesis, that lucidity founders in metaphor, that uncertainty is resolved in a work of art" (MS 20). Camus's remarks on science are brief and not sophisticated, yet they have the ring of the accepted Kuhnian assessment of science prevalent today. Western rationalism, with its encompassing explanations and essences behind appearances ("It is natural to give a clear view of the world after accepting the idea that it must be clear," MS 42), holds little interest for Camus, who is actively engaged with thinking through the "absurd sensitivity that can be found widespread in the age." In this context, he is more concerned with "the step taken by the mind when, starting from a philosophy of the world's lack of meaning, it ends up by finding a meaning and depth in it" (MS 42). This would be the thinking Camus refers to as "existentialist," represented foremost by Kierkegaard (although one can surely see Augustine in the background). According to Camus, Kierkegaard challenges the heart of Western rationalism by attacking the very demand for coherence, committing as it were "philosophical suicide." The hubris of human beings expressed in the desire to reduce the world to clarity is what Kierkegaard diagnoses as the problem. It is a sin against the creature's finitude. Countering the pretension of a reduction of the world to the human, the "leap" of faith expresses the creature's nothingness and total dependency on God. But, for Camus, the leap breaks the very tension constitutive of the human condition, resolving its antinomies, not in the typical rationalist fashion, but in what he views as an irrationalist end run:

> My reasoning wants to be faithful to the evidence that aroused it. That evidence is the absurd. It is the divorce between the mind that desires and the world that disappoints, my nostalgia for unity, this fragmented universe and the contradiction that binds them to-

gether. Kierkegaard suppresses my nostalgia and Husserl gathers together that universe. That is not what I was expecting. It was a matter of living and thinking with those dislocations. (MS 50)

Reason is an essential ingredient in the experience of the absurd, which would be dissolved with reason's dissolution. For Camus, reason "has its order in which it is efficacious. It is properly that of human experience" (MS 36). He unfortunately does not clarify. Presumably, reason is tightly bound to some sort of verification by lived bodily experience: "What can a meaning outside my condition mean to me? I can understand only in human terms. What I touch, what resists me—that is what I understand" (MS 51). The very fact that within its own modest limits reason is efficacious tempts one to believe in an unlimited reason, to transcend the "scale" of the *doxa* of life experience in the name of an unlimited, totalizing reason, or, on the other hand, to negate and humiliate reason altogether. Just as in *The Wrong Side and the Right Side,* where Camus placed himself "between yes and no," on this issue it is a question of "living and thinking with those dislocations."

We have already noted Camus's advertisement of his intentions in *The Myth of Sisyphus.* He is taking up an idea "widespread in the age." Looking back years later in *The Rebel,* he insisted that "the perception of the absurd is one perception among many. That it has colored so many thoughts and actions between the two wars only proves its power and validity. But the intensity of a perception does not necessarily mean that it is universal" (R 9). The absurd is one of a number of possible and legitimate paths of thinking about life. Husserl and Kierkegaard are not wrong. They simply do not meet the conditions that Camus has set up for his own thinking. Indeed, there is undisguised similarity between *The Myth of Sisyphus* and Descartes's *Meditations* in the use of methodic doubt and a first truth. But Camus's truth is not "logical." It is intensely personal: "What I know, what is certain, what I cannot deny, what I cannot reject—this is what counts. . . . What other truth can I admit without lying?" (MS 51). Camus's first truth, the absurd, is foundational, but only in the sense of picking up a contingent, cultural tool "widespread in the age" to employ as a "first beginning" in exploring his own life experience. The personal life experience expressed in the antinomies of *The Wrong Side and the Right Side* entangle creatively with the idea of the absurd in *The Myth of Sisyphus*. While admitting in *The Myth* "what these pages owe to certain contemporary thinkers," Camus does not simply repeat their views, but in appropriating them for his purposes gives them a new twist, what Merleau-Ponty would call a hermeneutic "deformation" of meaning, which appears in Camus's notion of rebellion.

"What," asks Camus, "does life mean in such a universe?" If the absurd is only a point of departure, what follows? "There is but one truly serious philosophical problem and that is suicide. Judging whether life is or is not worth living amounts to answering the fundamental question of philosophy" (MS 3). By the conditions Camus sets for himself, physical suicide, like philosophical suicide, would not be a "solution" of the absurd, but its dissolution, since "the absurd depends as much on man as on the world" (MS 21). Moreover, the absurd as a reason for suicide implies no logical entailment. It is crucial to recognize that the absurd is a relative notion for Camus. The absurd is a tension, born of a discrepancy between external reality and the human desire for familiarity. There is no total absurdity, for there exist beauty, friendship, health, fulfilling work. But on the other hand, these activities and dimensions of life are contingent, menaced constantly and doomed to end in death. Relative happiness and familiarity are possible. To commit suicide because of their relativity is to surrender all that is possible. It is to lose everything of the relative, which is really "the absolute" for it is all we humans have. The *doxa* of life are a weave of beauty and ugliness, friendship and misunderstanding, health and sickness, insight and opacity. It is a question of living with the mix and of not succumbing to the temptation of absolutizing either hope or despair. To rebel is to lucidly and courageously decide to live and "to exhaust the limits of the possible" by making the most out of life. Life is the value condition for all value; it must be accepted with its antinomies and treasured for its very fragility. "The point is to live." So ends *The Myth of Sisyphus,* whose personal origins echo *Le Rua*'s brief notice of the young goalie's absence from play.

## II

When the Allies landed in North Africa in November 1942, Camus was recuperating at Le Panelier in southern France from a recurrence of his tuberculosis (his left lung was found to be infected). He found himself cut off from his wife, who had just returned to Algeria, and without the job with *Paris-Soir* he had to abandon when the Germans occupied Paris. Friends managed to obtain some work for Camus reading manuscripts for the publishing house of Gallimard.[2] It was during this time in southern France that he met, through his friend Pascal Pia, members of the French Resistance. By the fall of 1943, Camus had moved back to Paris and joined the Combat movement of the Resistance. In August 1944 he became editor in chief of *Combat,* the movement's newspaper, with a subscription of around 250,000. He resigned his editorship and left the newspaper, which had continued publication after the war's end, on June 3, 1947.

Evidence of an effect of this new life experience on Camus's thought is apparent in his *Letters to a German Friend,* four letters to a fictitious German friend written between February and July 1944. Without being directly posed as it would be seven years later in *The Rebel,* the question that drives the *Letters* is that of the absurd and values: What happens to ethics and politics without their usual foundations available in rationalistic metaphysics and theology? The fourth letter culminates in something of an argument. Both Camus and his correspondent begin with the premise of the absurd, the lack of existence of "ultimate meaning," of familiarity between human desire and the universe. Both Camus and the German friend react by feeling "cheated." This particular reaction, crucial to the argument Camus is developing, implies the claim of being wronged, the idea that something is going on that should not be. In turn, this negative reaction implies a positive claim about what should be going on. If the absurd is the discrepancy between desire and the universe, and if it is that very discrepancy which causes one to feel wronged, then it is clear that what is "right," what "ought to be," is that human desire should be fulfilled instead of frustrated. The conclusion is, first, that the authentic rebel against the absurd ought never to add to the ab-

surd by increasing the misery consequent upon the separation between desire and reality, and second, that the authentic rebel
ought to heal as much as possible the wound or fissure between
desire and reality by drawing the two together as much as possible. There are degrees of the absurd. There are both inevitable
and needless sufferings and deaths. The rebel will recognize and
attend to the difference by never adding to, but on the contrary,
working to minimize, the absurd. The German friend is inconsis-
tent. (In the terms of *The Rebel,* Camus would say that the German friend betrays the very value in the name of which he
protests against the injustice of the absurd.) On the one hand, the
friend feels wronged and cheated by the absurd (implying that it
is unjust), while on the other hand, by colluding with the Nazis,
he increases the amount of suffering and death, thereby becoming
an agent of the absurd. "As you see, from the same principle we
derived quite different codes. . . . [Y]ou saw the injustice of our
condition to the point of being willing to add to it, whereas it
seemed to me that man must exalt justice in order to fight against
eternal injustice, create happiness in order to fight against the universe of unhappiness" (RRD 21). The German friend, beginning
with the absurd, concludes with "the idea that everything was
equivalent and that good and evil could be defined according to
one's wishes." Camus adds that "believing I thought as you did,"
he had "no argument to answer" his friend. Indeed, Camus's depiction of rebellion in *The Myth* is ambiguous about the moral
question. "On the one hand the absurd teaches that all experiences are unimportant, and on the other it urges toward the greatest quantity of experiences" (MS 62). Given the absurd, "the scale
of values becomes useless. . . . I must say that what counts is not
the best living but the most living. It is not up to me to wonder
if this is vulgar or revolting, elegant or deplorable. Once and for
all, value judgments are discarded here in favor of factual judgments" (MS 63). There is no issue here, in *The Myth,* of justifying
the killing of others, for the argument against suicide is premised
on life itself being the value that conditions all values. But Camus
does seem to propose that within this context, judgments of quality must yield to quantity: "There will never be any substitute
for twenty years of life and experience." Camus sees this as a
consequence of embracing the *doxa:* "For the absurd man . . . all

aspects of the world are privileged," so "to say that everything is privileged is tantamount to saying that everything is equivalent" (MS 45, 63).

What separates the meditation on revolt in *The Myth* from that in the *Letters* is the social dimension present in the latter. In *The Myth*, Camus appears to assume that his rejection of essentialism opens him to a world of nominalism, of sheer individualism. He rejects any "notion which eludes me and loses its meaning as soon as it goes beyond the frame of reference of my individual experience" (MS 56). Of "the weight of my own life," he says, "I must carry it alone." The absurd man will maintain the absurd "constantly by solitary effort" (MS 55). But the *Letters* appeal to human "solidarity": "Meanwhile, refusing to accept that despair and that tortured world, I merely wanted men to rediscover their solidarity in order to wage war against their revolting fate" (RRD 21). In fact, the entire argument of the *Letters* hinges on this notion of solidarity. The argument, if translated into the terms of *The Myth*, would have this logic: I experience the absurd (my unfamiliarity with the universe); I feel cheated, wronged; this implies that I ought not to be cheated and that *my* desires should be fulfilled, not frustrated; thus, I will be a rebel against the absurd by trying to match *my* desires with reality in the form of living as intensely as I can. But this form of the argument would not generate the conclusion that Camus requires to separate himself from his German friend. The argument will work to Camus's purpose only if my experience of the absurd, and my experience of being cheated, can lead to the further step that the *all people's* desires, not just my own, ought to be fulfilled, which will produce then the conclusion that the absurd should be diminished not just in my life, but in all lives. The argument will work only if there is some sort of identity or important linkage established between my life and others' lives. This is what his subsequent works, *The Plague* and *The Rebel*, seek to accomplish.

*The Plague* explores the movement from I to We. Camus notes that "in the early period of the plague" most citizens of Oran experienced the plague's impact in the "extremity of solitude," in which "none could count on any help from his neighbor; each had to bear the load of his troubles alone" (P 71). Each person was, as it were, submerged in individual feelings and concerns and

thereby a stranger to others. Communication "always missed fire"
for lack of finding "the truly expressive word" from "the current
coin of language, the commonplaces of plain narrative" (P 72).
Rambert, the visiting journalist investigating "the living-condi-
tions in the Arab quarter" and caught in the city's quarantine,
represents life in its I form, and indeed the nominalism of Camus's
early works. Perhaps the most telling scene in the novel occurs
when Rambert visits Dr. Rieux to obtain medical certification of
being free of the plague, in hope of leaving the town to which he
was a "stranger." Rieux, whose first response to the presence of
the plague was to turn his attention to its victims, can be read as
representing the socially committed form of rebellion sketched
out in the *Letters*. Two dimensions of Camus's own life experience and work debate with themselves in this scene. Rieux's response represents life in its We form: "I know its an absurd
situation, but we're all involved in it, and we've got to accept it
as it is" (P 81). To Rambert's response "I don't belong here,"
Rieux declares, "Unfortunately, from now on you'll belong here,
like everyone else" (P 82). Rieux is attempting to shatter the
nominalist and solitary stance of Rambert by insisting that Rambert is, "like everyone else," caught by the plague and, ultimately,
by the human (absurd) condition. One is not truly alone. Camus
will insist on this in *The Rebel* as the starting point for ethics and
politics: "The first progressive step for a mind overwhelmed by
the strangeness of things is to realize that this feeling is shared with
all men and that human reality, in its entirety, suffers from the
distance which separates it from the rest of the universe. The
malady experienced by a single man becomes a mass plague"
(R 22).

In the Resistance movement, Camus experienced the "camara-
derie of a struggle" born of a united effort by people of quite
different backgrounds and views. Writing in his *Notebooks* at this
time, he declares that "what links us to human beings" is "the
thing that lights up the world and makes it bearable" (N 57). In
his *Combat* articles he extols virtues of "generosity," "sacrifice,"
and "selflessness" as previously he praised lucidity, honesty, and
courage. It is in the light of this wartime experience that the I and
We are set in dramatic tension in *The Plague*. It is also not surpris-
ing that Rambert relents and takes the side of the We. Later in

the narrative Rambert returns to see Rieux to inform him that he is not leaving. "Until now," Rambert tells Rieux, "I always felt a stranger in this town, and that I'd no concern with you people. But now that I have seen what I have seen, I know only that I belong here whether I want it or not. This business is everybody's business" (P 188). Perhaps the scene that best celebrates and also demonstrates the turn to the We is that in which Rieux and Tarrou go swimming at the end of a difficult day: "For some minutes they swam side by side, with the same zest, in the same rhythm, isolated from the world, at last free of the town and of the plague. . . . They dressed and started back. Neither had said a word, but they were conscious of being perfectly at one, and the memory of this night would be cherished by them both" (P 233). The absurd is present insofar as both men are "isolated from the world." Yet, in contrast to this discrepant relationship, the two men swim "side by side . . . in the same rhythm . . . conscious of being perfectly at one." Human relationships do not have to suffer the "unfamiliarity" characteristic of the absurd relation of humans to the universe. The universe is inevitably silent and unresponsive to its human inhabitants, who are always strangers to it. But human beings can respond to other human beings, establish fellow feeling, and come to one another's aid. Community is possible and becomes the working ideal of Camus's ethics and politics. *Combat* continued its existence, under Camus's editorship, after the war, and in its pages and in Camus's imagination the Resistance experience would surpass the immediate conditions which spawned it to become the basis of a "new world order," an internationally cooperative unity of peoples: "We all know, then, beyond the shadow of a doubt, that the new world order we seek can be neither national nor even continental, and certainly not Western or Eastern" (BHR 129).

Whereas the *Letters* establishes the necessity of solidarity for ethical and political purposes, *The Plague* seeks a basis for solidarity in a shared condition in which participants are able to recognize themselves as alike. When Rieux tells Rambert that "it's an absurd situation, but we're all involved in it," the suggestion is that the exile of the inhabitants of Oran is a symbol for the common estrangement of all humans from the universe. In *The Rebel*, Camus would continue to explore human solidarity, but with a new twist: "In our daily trials rebellion plays the same role as does the '*cogito*' in the realm of thought: it is the first piece of evidence. But this evidence lures the individual from his solitude. It founds its first value on the whole human race. I rebel—therefore we exist" (R 22). His reference to the "human race" marks the taking up in *The Rebel* of the notion of a human nature: "Analysis of rebellion leads at least to the suspicion that, contrary to the postulates of contemporary thought, a human nature does exist, as the Greeks believed" (R 16). An act of rebellion is an individual act of protest, announcing that a certain limit has been reached. While on the surface a negation and a rejection, an act of rebellion is implicitly affirmative because the limit experience implies the discourse of value. The rebel protests because something of worth is threatened. The value invoked in rebellion, according to Camus, is not simply individual, but something "common to himself and to all men. . . . The affirmation implicit in every act of rebellion is extended to something that transcends the individual in so far as it withdraws him from his supposed solitude" (R 16). In this way the "limits" discovered in the individual experience of rebellion are transposed into universal "rights."

In his struggle to think an ethics starting from the absurd, especially by the attempt to ground solidarity in human nature, Camus is apparently contesting his earlier nominalism. To the Camus of *The Myth,* "the prestige of the real" belonged to "the concrete object of my attention, this sky, the reflection of that water on this coat" (MS 47). One recalls his claim that "thinking is not unifying or making the appearance familiar under the guise of the great principle" (MS 43). Aristotle's natures, as elements within the broader hylomorphic theory, would for the early Camus be just as much "constructs" as the planetary imagery he cites as involved in projecting an understanding of the atomic structure. And Descartes's self-intuition into the human essence is explicitly rejected: "For if I try to seize this self of which I feel sure, if I try to define and summarize it, it is nothing but water slipping through my fingers. . . . Between the certainty I have of my existence and the content I try to give to that assurance the gap will never be filled" (MS 19). In parody of Descartes, Camus articulates his own *cogito:* "Of whom and of what indeed can I say: 'I know that!' This heart within me I can feel, and I judge that it exists. This world I can touch, and I likewise judge that it exists. There ends all my knowledge, and the rest is construction" (MS 19). Despite his own admonitions and even within the modest limits of the essay, Camus breaks the boundaries of the merely autobiographical: "If I wish to limit myself to facts, I know what man wants, I know what the world offers him, and now I can say that I also know what links them. I have no need to dig deeper. A single certainty is enough for the seeker" (MS 30). The "certainty" here involves not just his own lived experience, his own "heart," but also the hearts of "man." Camus assumes that his own deepest aspirations are an example of "man's unconscious feeling in the face of his universe: it is an insistence upon familiarity" (MS 17). Granted that *The Myth* is an experiment, an attempt to take up an idea (the absurd) and thoroughly think it through, and that this thinking is thoroughly personal, even within these parameters Camus fails to come to grips with his professed nominalism and his general claims. If he could ignore this issue in *The Myth,* he could no longer do so in *The Letters, The Plague,* and *The Rebel,* where he is convinced that solidarity is essential for the viability of his notions of ethics and politics.

While Camus appeals, in *The Rebel,* to a common human nature to ground solidarity, his understanding of that notion is not deeply metaphysical. Totally absent are projections of particular behavioral patterns as are customarily found among advocates of human nature. Rather, Camus speaks of "a common destiny," of "a common texture, the solidarity of chains, a communication between human being and human being which makes men both similar and united" (R 283, 282). Suffering, death, and speech are mentioned most often as constituting the "common texture." It is true that Camus thinks that human nature sets limits, that people are not infinitely malleable. "Nature" becomes "limit" in the claim that the rebel makes. The limit is available to us only in the protest of the rebel, who, in crying out, is invoking a value, making a demand or claim, and seeking a response. Nature, to appear as limit, must be *felt* or *experienced* as breached in order to become morally intelligible.

The appeal to a common human nature is inseparable from dialogue's necessary role in defining the ethical and political meaning of that appeal.[3] The rebel's claim for response continues

Camus's commitment, declared in *The Plague,* to the possibility of creating a unity among people, of not allowing human relationships to be overcome with absurdity as reflected in the universe's silence or indifference to human suffering. Dialogue is a principal antidote to the absurd insofar as by means of it solidarity is both recognized and established. For Camus, people are similar because they share a common lot of suffering and death, but solidarity in the full sense is established only when this common lot is recognized:

> There is, in fact, nothing in common between a master and a slave; it is impossible to speak and communicate with a person who has been reduced to servitude. Instead of the untrammeled dialogue through which we come to recognize our similarity and consecrate our destiny, servitude gives way to the most terrible of silences. If injustice is bad for the rebel, it is not because it contradicts an eternal idea of injustice, but because it perpetuates the silent hostility that separates the oppressor from the oppressed. It kills the small part of existence that can be realized on this earth through the mutual understanding of men. . . . The mutual understanding and communication discovered by rebellion can survive only in the free exchange of conversation. (R 283)

"The silent hostility that separates the oppressor from the oppressed" is precisely the presence of the absurd in human relationships. The rebel, feeling cheated by the absurd, and as one committed to fight the absurd, will work to open lines of communication and foster conditions of dialogue. The rebel discovers value, not in the "eternal idea," but "in the heat of battle and in the incessant movement of contradiction" (R 283), that is, in experiences of suffering and oppression. Rebellion must "find its reasons within itself." Yet, central and indispensable as it is to Camus's project, rebellion is itself a contingent, historical ground. Rebellion is just one possible response to suffering and death, and it has appeared under certain historical conditions: "The problem of rebellion seems to assume a precise meaning only within the confines of Western thought. . . . The spirit of rebellion can exist only in a society where a theoretical equality conceals great factual inequalities. The problem of rebellion, therefore, has no meaning except within our own Western society" (R 20). Significantly, rebellion, for Camus, is a secular, as opposed to sacred, response to the human condition, one in which "all the answers are human." Camus must start where he is, and he told us where he is in *The Myth:* "What can a meaning outside my condition mean to me? I can understand only in human terms. . . . What other truth can I admit without lying, without bringing in a hope I lack and which means nothing within the limits of my condition?" (MS 51).

Camus's attempts to think through an ethics and politics—the difficulties he encounters as well as his responses—are, on a number of counts, echoed today in the work of Richard Rorty. Rorty addresses himself to ethics and politics as a nominalist antimetaphysician, establishing himself with those credentials in *Philosophy and the Mirror of Nature.*[4] In subsequent work he examines the consequences for life which might follow the deconstruction of metaphysics. One consequence of the removal of metaphysical grounds for Rorty is the recovery of life as a work of art. Individuals find themselves embedded in contingent narratives on the basis of which the self weaves a life. Truly creative individuals recognize the contingency of narratives to the point of being able to rewrite or redescribe their lives and to thereby become models of possibility for others. The "ironist," according to Rorty, is "the sort of person who faces up to the contingency of his or her own most central beliefs and desires—someone sufficiently historicist and nominalist to have abandoned the idea that those central beliefs and desires refer back to something beyond the reach of time and chance."[5] Given the absence of any "final vocabulary" in which reality and self find definition, there exists a multiplicity of narratives about reality and self. Ironists such as Nietzsche, Sartre, Derrida, and Foucault are heroes for Rorty for showing up the contingent nature of purportedly necessarily grounded narratives about life and for being examples of those who would creatively renarrate life. Camus's absurd hero shares these "ironic" characteristics. Lucidity about the absurdity of life has a "liberating" effect, freeing one up, Camus says, for one's passion. One breaks out of "the habit of living" into "exhausting the limits of the possible." Nietzsche is clearly present in both Rorty's ironist and Camus's absurd hero. Yet, Nietzsche becomes a problem for both thinkers when they turn to ethics and politics, where, for them, solidarity holds central place.

Rorty sees his ironist philosophical heroes as "invaluable in our attempt to form a private self-image," but "irrelevant to public life and to political questions . . . pretty much useless when it comes to politics."[6] Public space involves solidarity, a sense of We. But this solidarity is postmetaphysical, not founded upon the deep structure of a "core self" or a given human essence. Non-metaphysical solidarity is contingent, and refers only to the happenstance of being born into a family, tribe, or nation, sharing a particular form of common life and language with others. Solidarity is a historical/social creation. Since there is, for Rorty, no metaphysical foundation for ethics or politics, the latter are simply found in one's historical/social situation. Since there are many different such situations, there are many different forms of ethics and politics, with no hope (metaphysical or theological) of making an objective determination of truth in their regard. Absent absolute truth as correspondence of one's ideas with reality, the only available truth is "the idea of truth as what comes to be believed in the course of free and open encounters."[7] An ironist himself, Rorty is aware that his own ethical and political views are held on the basis of his own historical/social formation. He identifies himself as a "liberal," one committed to the reduction of pain and suffering (particularly in the form of the pain of "humiliation"). Historically, this view evolved in "Europe and America in the last 300 years" and is a vocabulary "typical of the secularized democratic societies of the West." Rorty, while aware of the contingency of his ethical/political beliefs, judges that they are the best available since "contemporary liberal society already contains the institutions for its own improvement. . . . Indeed, my hunch is that Western social and political thought may have had the last *conceptual* revolution it needs."[8] While Nietzsche is Rorty's ironist hero, J. S. Mill is his liberal ironist hero.

In *The Rebel,* Camus comes to terms with Nietzsche, his absurd hero, in the context of ethics and politics, and finds him dangerous. While Camus identifies with Nietzsche's critique of Western metaphysics, with its pretension of transcending the sensible world and bodies, he finds problematic what he reads as Nietzsche's affirmation of and consent to "the innocence of the ceaseless change of things": "This magnificent consent, born of abundance and fullness of spirit, is the unreserved affirmation of human imperfection and suffering, of evil and murder, of all that is problematic and strange in our existence" (R 72). Nietzsche's rebellion, on behalf of this world and of appearance, is just fine. However, Camus thinks that Nietzsche's affirmation affirms too much. Camus's rebel, within the *doxa* itself, in the experience of suffering, discovers a limit, proclaims an injustice. Suffering, while inevitable, is to be fought, limited, contained. Healing, offering the hand to the weak and helpless, is to be promoted. Dialogue and democracy are to be nourished and institutionalized. Nietzsche as absurd hero is to be replaced by the Resistance fighter and trade unionist, those who are committed to fighting needless oppression in solidarity with fellow sufferers. But, as we have noted, rebellion itself is a historically contingent phenomenon, an attitude of the secular West, "a society where a theoretical equality conceals great factual inequalities." Rorty puts it similarly when he says that the liberal is "protesting in the name of the society itself against those aspects of the society which are unfaithful to its own self-image."[9]

Rorty is suspicious of the universal: "A universalistic ethics seems incompatible with ironism, simply because it is hard to imagine stating such an ethic without some doctrine about the nature of man."[10] Yet he is not content with the ethnocentrist We:

> On the other hand, my position is *not* incompatible with urging that we try to extend our sense of "we" to people whom we have previously thought of as "they." . . . The view that I am offering says that there is such a thing as moral progress, and that this progress is indeed in the direction of greater human solidarity. But that solidarity is not thought of as a recognition of a core self, the human essence, in all human beings. Rather, it is thought of as the ability to see more and more traditional differences (of tribe, religion, race, customs, and the like) as unimportant when compared with similarities with respect to pain and humiliation—the ability to think of people wildly different from ourselves as included in the range of "us."[11]

Solidarity, then, is a task for Rorty, something to be created, not "something that exists antecedently to our recognition of it." Rorty's nominalism denies the existence of metaphysically given unities such as natures or essences. Yet he does appeal to "similarities" among people, for the liberal ironist "thinks that what unites her to the rest of the species is not a common language but *just* susceptibility to pain and in particular to that special sort of pain which the brutes do not share with the humans—humiliation."[12] The "fact" that people suffer does not in itself, as it were, constitute a solidarity among the suffering, for solidarity implies an act of recognition and identification. For Rorty, liberals are those who engage in such recognition and identification, along with moral indignation about suffering and a commitment to lessen it. We have seen that Camus, while employing the term "human nature," grants it a weak sense, usually the sense that human beings share a common lot of death and suffering. It is clear, for Camus, that such common features, although "natural," await recognition before being incorporated into solidarity. He writes of "the implicit and untrammeled dialogue through which we come to recognize our similarity and consecrate our destiny" (R 283). For Camus, apparently, as for Rorty, an act of identification with the other is crucial for the emergence of solidarity, and both believe, in theory, that through dialogue/conversation a solidarity that transcends one's ethnocentrism is possible. Both thinkers are convinced that in this way, without a metaphysical foundation, Enlightenment values can be sustained.

Camus and Rorty are both up-front about their contingent grounding in Western values and, in particular, liberal values. Where else is one expected to begin thinking about ethics/politics, they would ask us, than in one's historical/cultural place? The We that one begins with is always a particular We, but a We that is open to expansion. Since notions such as "Western values" and "liberalism" are themselves not metaphysical essences, they ought to be contested sites. Camus's view that liberalism's exemplar is Scandinavian socialism, and his distrust of technology, do contest Rorty's contentment with "bourgeois liberalism." There is, however, a tension, perhaps not fully appreciated by each thinker, between their purportedly contingent initial commitments and their more expansive hopes. Camus, because of his appeal to a common humanity in *The Plague* and *The Rebel,* was perceived by some critics to be a moralizing spokesperson of the universal, assuming in the eyes of his critics the role of the voice of humanity. Indeed, Camus defended himself from criticism of

*The Rebel* with the preface that he was speaking not in his name, but in the name of human freedom. Critics have noticed the absence of Arabs from the We of plague fighters in Oran as well as Camus's exclusion of non-Westerners from participation in revolt (ironically at the same time that Arabs in his homeland were conducting armed insurrection). Rorty pulls no punches: "J. S. Mill's suggestion that governments devote themselves to optimizing the balance between leaving people's private lives alone and preventing suffering seems to me pretty much the last word."[13] In other contexts Rorty has eschewed "final vocabularies," but here he endorses something like a final word. The contingent We is not only an initially unavoidable starting point, but, it appears, an ending point as well, which makes the notions of Camusian dialogue and Rortian conversation somewhat problematic. One expects from the positing of a metaphysical ground claims that bind necessarily and (despite appearances) universally; one does not expect this from contingent/historical grounds. Rather, one would expect a sense of We that is always troubled, constantly in question, open to interpretation and future reformulation. Since meanings are not pinned down by essences, the very meaning of the basic terms in liberal discourse—"freedom," "private" and "public," "harm"—should be themselves open to constant negotiation. We can see that the question of identity for Camus and Rorty, even as it is freed from its fixity in metaphysics, remains problematic for both as they articulate the place of solidarity in their ethics and politics. Tendencies toward assuming an intractable givenness of the We translate into attitudes of assimilation of alterity to the detriment of dialogue and conversation. This was evident for some time in Camus's assessment of colonialism in his homeland.

### III

Early in 1956, Camus returned to Algeria to plead with all sides for a truce to the increasingly bloody internal conflict in his homeland. The French government had warned him that he would be in danger. As he entered the hall near the Casbah where he was to speak, from out of the crowd of thousands of French

Algerian (*pieds noirs*) demonstrators he heard shouts of "Camus to the gallows." Inside the hall Camus addressed a full house divided evenly between French Algerians and Moslems.

> White-faced and clenching his sheaf of papers he read, too rapidly to be heard. He repeated what he had said so often. He had "lived the Algerian tragedy like a personal tragedy." He had "more doubt than certainties to express" but he was certain that nothing could come from violence. The civilian truce was self-evidently good and might be a step towards a broader compromise. Outside the shouts of "Camus to the gallows" grew louder and inside the hall the listeners grew more tense. The nervous Camus stumbled through his last lines, sat down and told Robles, who was acting as chairman, to wind up the meeting.[14]

In 1939, as a young reporter for *Alger-republicain,* Camus wrote a series of articles, "Misère de la Kabylie," on the plight of Arab victims of famine in the Kabylia region of Algeria. In eleven installments, Camus depicted the enormous suffering inflicted upon these people by the French/Algerian government's policies, and suggested needed reforms. He did not condemn the colonial system, but rather appealed to metropolitan France to take the lead in initiating reform, because the local government had repeatedly caved in to the influence of wealthy French *colons*. Camus's articles, which appeared in April, contributed to the Algerian government's ban on his newspaper's publication the following January. Toward the end of the war (October 1944), he brought up the issue of the French colonies in North Africa in *Combat,* advising the metropolitan government that "as we seek to extend the political enfranchisement that the provisional government has bestowed on the natives of North Africa, we must recognize that the worst obstacle will be the French population" (BHR 65). Camus is maintaining his concern with colonial exploitation and encouraging full assimilation of the native populations: "We will find support from our colonies only when we have convinced them that their interests are our interests and that we do not have contrary policies, one giving justice to the French people, the other consecrating injustice in our empire" (BHR 65). French inaction and famine conditions contributed to an outbreak of violence in Algeria, at Sétif, in March 1945. Arabs killed some European Algerians, and in reprisal, thousands of Arabs were killed. At the time Camus was in Algeria, and he used the occasion for a fact-finding excursion of three weeks and fifteen hundred miles across Algeria, the results of which he published in a series of articles in *Combat*. Conditions had worsened since his earlier reports on famine in Kabylia. Moreover, it was now clear that the Arab population was not interested in assimilation, but instead desired independence. Undeterred, Camus doggedly argued that the situation could still be saved by a massive effort to do "justice" to the Arabs, immediately by getting them food (their official food rations were below those of prewar days and much below the rations of European Algerians), and by implementing the suggestions for reform he had made years earlier, including full enfranchisement: "It is the humble force of justice, and it alone which must help us to reconquer Algeria and its inhabitants."[15] By the time Camus delivered his appeal for a truce in 1956 to the cries of "Camus to the gallows," positions had so hardened and violence had so escalated that he was considered an outsider to the majority populations of Arabs and French Algerians.

Camus's persistence in arguing for assimilation for the Arabs, as well as his reluctance to initially condemn wholesale the colonial system, reflects his *pied noir* identity as a fourth-generation French Algerian on his father's side and a fourth-generation Spanish Algerian on his mother's. Camus considered Algeria his homeland. When he did come to condemn the colonial system and to recognize the native independence movements in French colonies such as Tunisia, he made an exception in Algeria's case because of the number of European settlers. The Arab population of Algeria in the 1950s was over eight million, while the European population was over one million. In the midst of the increased violence of the 1950s, Camus wrote: "Recognizing the end of colonialism, my solution excludes dreams of reconquest or of maintaining the status quo. . . . But my solution also excludes the dream of uprooting the French in Algeria who, if they have no right to oppress anyone, do have a right not to be oppressed themselves" (RRD 89, 90). The injustice of colonialism must be addressed, so he argued, but not by "substituting one injustice for another." Camus's insistence on the "justice" of the cause of the French Algerians separated him from most of his left-wing colleagues in

France, such as Sartre, for whom the violence perpetrated by both sides should not be considered on equal terms. Camus's response to this sort of criticism displayed his particularist involvement in the struggle: "When violence answers violence in a growing frenzy that makes the simple language of reason impossible, the role of intellectuals cannot be, as we read everyday, to excuse from a distance one of the violences and condemn the other. . . . When the fate of men and women of one's own blood is bound, directly or indirectly, to the articles one writes in the comfort of the study, one has the right to hesitate and to weigh the pros and cons" (RRD 84, 82). Camus condemned "with equal force and no uncertain terms" the violence of both sides, taking his stand "in the no-man's land between two armies and preaching amid the bullets that war is a deception" (RRD 92).

Camus's initial nominalism wavered and gave way, in the light of his experience in the Resistance, to solidarity and a possible unification of peoples beyond what divided them. "It's an absurd situation," Dr. Rieux declares to Rambert, "but we're all involved in it." While Rieux does not at all share Fr. Paneloux's theology of suffering, he is able to tell him that "We're working side by side for something that unites us—beyond blasphemy and prayers. And it's the only thing that matters" (P 203). Solidarity emerges in this "beyond" of differences, a unity (We) confirmed on the recognition of a sameness of, or commonly shared aspect of, certain features of the human condition, depicted in the imagery of Rieux and Tarrou swimming "side by side . . . in the same rhythm . . . conscious of being perfectly at one." The difficulty of his position lay in balancing the tension between appeals to an existing human nature as universal ground on the one hand and to dialogue as an incorporation of viewpoints in establishing common ground and mutual understanding on the other. While appeals to commonalities are a strategy for gaining mutual recognition, the commonalities must themselves be recognized. The danger is to assume that one's own insertion in commonalities means the same thing to others. One cannot assume, without consulting them, that the fact that various people are mortal means sufficiently the same thing to automatically constitute significant common ground. In his writings on the Algerian crisis, Camus is compelled to recognize his own particularity, with the result that he nuances his understanding of solidarity by way of highlighting differences, not in a return to his former nominalism, but in a heightened emphasis upon dialogue in the forging of universality in an open process. In his writing, Camus clearly identifies himself as French Algerian. He claims, for example, referring to brutalities committed by the French Algerian military, that "military combat and repression have, *on our side,* taken on aspects that we cannot accept" (RRD 83; emphasis added). In his "Letter to an Algerian Militant" he addresses "you Arabs" by way of reference to "us French liberals," but as well, with the Arab, he refers to "our country," composed of "two populations, similar and different at the same time but equally worthy of respect" (RRD 98). While the French Algerians have a right to belong in Algeria, they have no right "to destroy the roots of Arab culture and life." French and Arab "must live together at the crossroads where history has put them," but their differences ought not divide them. "As for me," Camus insists, "here as in every domain, I believe only in differences and not in uniformity."[16] Absent is all talk of assimilation and defense of a political We formed on the basis of already assumed shared identity. "I cannot," he admits, "speak in the name of our Arab friends" (RRD 100).

Before his death and the resolution of the Algerian crisis, Camus gave his approval to the ill-fated Lauriol Plan, which was devised "to respect particularisms and . . . to associate the two populations in the administration of their common interest" (RRD 108). "Association" is carefully distinguished from "fusing together." The plan envisaged a Parliament elected by proportional representation and divided into Houses, one of which would place Moslems in charge of "all questions involving Moslems and them alone," another that would involve French responsibility for laws "applying solely to the French," while matters "concerning the two communities" would be taken up by the full Parliament. Camus comments: "Contrary to all our practices, contrary above all to the deep-rooted prejudices inherited from the French Revolution, we should thus have sanctioned within the Republic two equal but distinct categories of citizens. From this point of view, this would mark a sort of revolution against the regime of centralization and abstract individualism resulting from 1789" (RRD 109). The "abstract individualism" of

the Enlightenment considers all individuals to be "equal" in the
sense of "the same." But "sameness" is an abstraction. Not all
French Algerians were the same, and few thought as Camus did
(the crowd that cried out "Camus to the gallows" was French
Algerian). Rejection of sameness (and essences) would imply
nominalism only for metaphysicians, not for philosophers committed to the *doxa,* where similarities and differences weave
throughout phenomena. A politics of the *doxa* recognizes similarities in the form of equalities and rights, which in turn are intelligible only in the context of differences. "Differences are the roots
without which the tree of liberty, the sap of creation and of civili-
zation, dries up" (RRD 98). Camus criticized the French Algerians for considering themselves to be the universal, excluding the
Arab Other from humanity, while he criticized the excluded
Arabs for absolutizing their particularity to the point of denying
accommodation. Both groups thereby were contributing to killing "the small part of existence that can be realized on this earth
through the mutual understanding of men" (R 284). It was in the
spirit of defending an ideal of nonreductive universality that
Camus thus spoke of "two populations, similar and different and
the same time and equally deserving of respect." The Lauriol Plan
recognized both difference and similarity, the latter in the different groups deliberating about matters "concerning the two communities." It is here that could grow, as opposed to an
assimilationist We, a concrete sense of a multiplicitous We, not
based upon an acceptance of an assumed sameness but opening a
space where common interest can forge bonds. If earlier circumstances in his life had motivated Camus to at one time privilege
difference (his life-threatening illness) and at another similarity
(the Resistance), his agonizing experience over the crisis in his
homeland gave him the opportunity to think them together.

Camus's philosophy is based upon a discrepancy embedded in
his experience of the world, a discrepancy productive of life experience itself: "If I were a tree among trees, a cat among animals,
this life would have a meaning, or rather this problem would not
arise, for I should belong to this world. I should *be* this world to
which I am now opposed by my whole consciousness and my
whole insistence upon familiarity" (MS 51). If the discrepancy

were to disappear, so would the self and its experience. The discrepancy breaks all fusion of self and reality and produces multiple experiences. The danger that haunts the self is that of seeking to overcome its own separation from reality in forms of fusion, in totality, seeking what would be its own death, in physical suicide, philosophical suicide, in totalitarian social temptations. Camus responded at first by conceiving a life project of thoroughly and unreservedly celebrating experiments with diverse constructions of lifestyle, and then, given his war experiences, by the creation of dialogical forms of community. In this latter project, his often painful attempt to imagine forms of unity which are dialogical and open while at the same time avoiding the impasses of nominalism and totality serves to create a new audience for his work in our postmodern times.

## Works of Camus Cited

BHR    *Between Hell and Reason: Essays from the Resistance Newspaper "Combat," 1944–1947.* Ed. and trans. Alexandre de Granant. Hanover, N.H.: University Press of New England, 1991.

LCE    *Lyrical and Critical Essays.* Trans. Ellen Kennedy. New York: Vintage Books, 1970 (*L'Envers et l'endroit.* Angiers: Charlot, 1937).

MS    *The Myth of Sisyphus.* Trans. Justin O'Brien. New York: Vintage Books, 1991 (*Le Mythe de Sisyphe.* Paris: Gallimard, 1942).

N    *Notebooks, 1942–1951.* Trans. Justin O'Brien. New York: Harvest Books, 1965 (*Carnets.* Vol. 2, *Jan. 1942–Mar. 1951.* Paris: Gallimard, 1964).

P    *The Plague.* Trans. Stuart Gilbert. New York: Vintage, 1972 (*La Peste.* Paris: Gallimard, 1947).

R    *The Rebel.* Trans. Anthony Bower. New York: Vintage International, 1991 (*L'Homme revolté.* Paris: Gallimard, 1951).

RRD    *Resistance, Rebellion, and Death.* Trans. Justin O'Brien. New York: Knopf, 1960.

## NOTES

I am grateful to David Sprintzen for the suggestions he offered me as I was preparing this piece.

1. Herbert Lottman, *Albert Camus* (New York: Doubleday, 1979), chapter 4.

2. Ibid., chapters 20–23.

3. David Sprintzen, in *Albert Camus: A Critical Examination* (Phila-delphia: Temple University Press, 1988), writes: "*The Rebel* thus focuses upon the limitations intrinsic to the effort to establish an intersubjective frame of reference for value claims. Such claims constitute a demand upon the other for acknowledgment. They must be justified and de-fended. What is to be their ground? Ultimately I shall maintain—along with Camus—that a claim becomes intersubjectively justifiable only as a proposal. It is an invitation to dialogue" (131). The "universality of content" of the appeal to human nature must, according to Sprintzen, "be progressively approached . . . only with and through the particular life of dialogic communities" (134).

4. Richard Rorty, *Philosophy and the Mirror of Nature* (Princeton, N.J.: Princeton University Press, 1979).

5. Richard Rorty, *Contingency, Irony, and Solidarity* (New York: Cambridge University Press, 1989), xv.

6. Ibid., 83.

7. Ibid., 68.

8. Ibid., 63.

9. Ibid., 60.

10. Ibid., 88.

11. Ibid., 192.

12. Ibid., 92.

13. Ibid., 63.

14. Patrick McCarthy, *Camus* (New York: Random House, 1982), 284.

15. Quoted in Lottman, *Camus,* 355.

16. Quoted in Sprintzen, *Camus,* 259.

## WORKS CONSULTED

Isaacs, Jeffrey. *Arendt, Camus, and Modern Rebellion.* New Haven, Conn.: Yale University Press, 1992.

Lottman, Herbert. *Albert Camus.* New York: Doubleday, 1979.

McCarthy, Patrick. *Camus.* New York: Random House, 1982.

Parker, Emmett. *Albert Camus: The Artist in the Arena.* Madison: University of Wisconsin Press, 1965.

Rorty, Richard. *Contingency, Irony, and Solidarity.* New York: Cambridge University Press, 1989.

———. *Philosophy and the Mirror of Nature.* Princeton, N.J.: Princeton University Press, 1979.

Sprintzen, David. *Albert Camus: A Critical Examination.* Philadelphia: Temple University Press, 1988.

Tarrow, Susan. *Exile from the Kingdom: A Political Rereading of Albert Camus.* Tuscaloosa: University of Alabama Press, 1985.

Walzer, Michael. *The Company of Critics: Social Criticism and Political Commitment in the Twentieth Century.* New York: Basic Books, 1988.

# 2

# Gabriel Marcel:
# Reflection as Interpretation

IN A NOTE OF JANUARY 7, 1914, in the beginning of his *Metaphysical Journal,* Gabriel Marcel writes that "the problems by which I am occupied at present are for the most part problems of method" (MJ 2). At the time he was intent on "avoiding both realism and pure subjectivism" in opening an intelligible space for religious faith. Many years later, thinking back upon his efforts, Marcel offered this assessment: "In rereading these already dated texts, I have the feeling that I was nonetheless still dominated at that time by the spirit of abstraction I have never ceased fighting since then, and indeed even then I was tempted to recognize the limits of idealism. All the same, it was as an idealist that I was speaking."[1] One of his idealist assumptions regarded his lack of appreciation for "the immediate," which at the time he equated with the un-intelligible: "From the standpoint of immediate experience nothing can be explained or even understood. . . . The immediate is the very reverse of the principle of intelligibility" (MJ 1). Since it was empiricism, he thought, that appealed to the immediate, it was idealism to which he must look for a corrective. Knowledge cannot be given in realistic fashion through a process in which the mind would receive content from immediate experience, because "thought cannot really have an internal content unless it gives it to itself, that is to say, unless it mediates that which is given to it as external" (MJ 113). The application of thought to experience is the bringing to experience of general conditions of intelligibility, constituting experience into "objectivity," the very condition of knowability. Existence is knowable only by the penetration into it of the mind's own categories. The notion of truth follows upon intelligibility: "To speak of truth regarding what is outside of existence is a contradiction in terms" (MJ 29). With this view of intelligibility in place, Marcel attempts to make room for religious faith by posing several aporias. How can the mind arise to an awareness of its functioning (its limits) if its knowledge is solely defined by its categories? Must not the mind transgress its categories to display their limits? How can non–temporal and necessary claims about the functioning of the mind be reconciled with the categorical functioning of the mind, which is temporally bound? Having committed himself to an idealist framework, Marcel is groping to loosen its hold on all forms of cognition.

To his credit, Marcel keeps pushing and questioning his own analyses until the reader soon senses a dramatic change of tone in the *Metaphysical Journal*. In an entry of May 1, 1920, he acknowledges his "evolution in the direction of realism," but also admits that he "cannot see where it is heading" (MJ 238). What moved him in his "realistic" direction was his probing of "participant experience" over against the sense of the "general conditions of intelligibility" which formerly, for him, defined intelligibility. Marcel noted that the body as it is lived affectively, *my body,* is not at all intelligible in terms of the general conditions of objectivity. The level of existence, now designated as that of immediate participation, is one wherein the subject/object categories subtending idealism are out of place. Objectification by reflection would not render, as Marcel previously held, existence to be intelligible, but would rather distort something that is, by its nature, resistant to objective analysis. He finally admits in a note of February 2, 1922, that he has reached a point where he must "effect a radical dissociation between the ideas of existence and objectivity" (MJ 231). The *Metaphysical Journal* would be published in 1927, the same year as Heidegger's *Being and Time,* but in 1925 Marcel published an article, "Existence and Objectivity" (appended as well to his *Metaphysical Journal*), summarizing his break with idealism. In it he singles out Descartes as representative of modernity's characteristic subject/object dualism and its presumption of the primacy of the epistemological subject created by the *cogito:*

> The reality that the *cogito* reveals—though without discovering an analytical basis for it—is of quite a different order from the existence we are trying here not so much to *establish* as to *identify.* . . .
> The *cogito* introduces us into a whole system of affirmations and

guarantees their validity. *It guards the threshold of the valid.* . . . But it certainly does not follow from this that the objective world to which access is opened up to us by the *cogito* coincides with the world of existence. (MJ 325)

Against the constructionist metaphors used by Descartes, such as building on secure ground and with solid foundations, Marcel counters with archaeological metaphors of digging and sifting. The point is not to find a more secure ground than Descartes's, but to find a level beneath the *cogito* where one encounters the sifting and insecure soil of contingent bodily life. "Doubt," Marcel writes (in regard to Descartes's method doubt), "is at least a provisional and recognized rupture of a particular attachment or adhesion; it is a 'disengagement' and hence it can be exercised after the event" (MJ 321). "Attachment," "adhesion," and "event" mark the praxis of existence, bodily, sensuous, and social insofar as lived or participated. The mistake of modern idealism (and modern realism as well) is to presume as valid method what is really "an arbitrary act by which thought claims to transform into an affirmation of objectivity what is really immediate apprehension and participation" (MJ 324).

*Being and Having,* the continuation of his journal entries from 1928 to 1933, and his essay "On the Ontological Mystery" (1933) record Marcel's struggle to develop a mode of thinking adept to deal with participant experience, resulting in his distinction between primary and secondary reflection. Primary reflection pretends to objectivity by assuming an impersonal, impartial, or neutral subjectivity, one that would abstract from participant experience of situatedness. He was enormously suspicious of this commitment to modern methodology: "Thought cannot go beyond existence; it can only in some degree abstract from it, and it is of the first importance that it should not be deceived by this act of abstraction" (BH 27). He contested the value-free declarations of such methodology and was a consistent critic of the impact of such thinking "beyond strictly limited purposes" in producing, through technology, a certain modern, passive, and uncreative type of person. Secondary reflection derives from the recognition that "thought is *inside* existence" (BH 27), a fact that poses serious problems, for if "knowledge is conditioned by a participation in

being for which no epistemology can account because it continually presupposes it," with the result that "participation cannot be,
by definition, an *object* of thought" (PE 18), then how can one
think existence at all without betraying it?

   In *Being and Having,* as Marcel was developing his views on
secondary reflection, he was dialoguing with certain Thomists.
While admitting to "all the misery I feel when I am confronted
with the Thomist claims" (BH 25), he did single out his agreement with them on the question of realism, that is, with the view
that one knows things and not one's own ideas. Much has been
made of this realist sympathy, particularly to the end of making
something of a Thomist of Marcel. Yet when this question is ex-
amined closely, I believe it is clear that Marcel's "realism" must
be judged to differ considerably from the Thomists'. In fact, in
forming his views on secondary reflection, Marcel employed,
quite consciously, the Platonic word "recollection," and would
admit only to "neo-Socratic" (a term he suggested) as a general
characterization of his thinking. Yet his thinking is no more Platonic in the usual sense than it is Thomist. The core of Marcel's
realism is the nonnegotiable irreducibility of thought's Other:
"To assert the immanence of thought in Being is to recognize the
reality that thought, as soon as it is there, refers to something that
transcends it and which it cannot claim to reabsorb into itself
without betraying its true nature" (BH 36). Indeed, Marcel asserts, thought transcends itself toward what is Other; it is "the
pursuit of the Other" (BH 30). However, what he means by the
relation to the irreducible Other has to be nuanced within the
qualifications of his theory of intuition: "It seems to me that I am
bound to admit that I am—anyway on one level of myself—face
to face with Being. In a sense I see it. In another sense, I cannot
say that I see it since I cannot grasp myself in the act of seeing it.
*The intuition is not, and cannot be, directly reflected in consciousness*"
(BH 98; emphasis added). There is a blind spot in thought which
precludes closure of thought upon itself, inevitable escape of
thought from self-identity. Knowledge of reality (Being) will be,
for Marcel, indirect. Secondary reflection is defined as "a thinking
which *stretches out* towards the recovery of an intuition which
otherwise loses itself in proportion as it is exercised." It "is a recovery, but only in so far as it remains tributary of what I have

called a blindfold intuition" (BH 118, 121). Secondary reflection finds its guide in intuition, but intuition is blind (because immediate) and must find its expression and articulation mediately. "Everything seems to go on as if I found myself acting on an intuition which I possess already without knowing myself to possess it—an intuition which cannot be, strictly speaking, self-conscious and which *can grasp itself only through the modes of experience in which its image is reflected,* and which it lights up by being thus reflected in them" (BH 118; emphasis added). Marcel's vocabulary is ambiguous, borrowing as it does from sources it strains against. "Intuition," "recovery" (and loss), and "image" conjure a nostalgia for origins, the loss of the promised land of Being and subsequent life in the wilderness of appearances. My view is, however, that Marcel is caught in the historical bind typical of many existentialists who were snagged by the very discourses they vigorously criticized. It is possible, and I think appropriate, to recognize from our present vantage the field of thought they actually were opening to us in a more generous reading of their works. The "recovery" alluded to by Marcel is not the work of producing a copy of what already exists. Marcel's realism is not that of traditional representationalism. This is clear from his insistence that the "subject" mediates between intuition and expression. "Let us admit," he says, "that Being has first laid a siege to the self; by this self I mean the subject that affirms. This subject none the less *intervenes between being and the affirmation,* in the role of mediator" (BH 140; emphasis added). To understand is to place what is to be understood in a framework that gives it meaning. This is the role of the situated self, which, because of its situatedness, is constrained to use expressive capacities, the contingent categories of meaning, borrowed from (or produced by) that very situatedness. The subject, for Marcel, is not external to its situation and its expressive capacities, presiding through "an already existing structure" (such as an objective human nature): "The very note of our human condition is, in fact, that it is not assimilable to some kind of objective and already existing structure which we have merely to uncover and explore. The human condition . . . seems to be in some ways dependent on the manner in which it is understood" (MM 98). This makes secondary reflection inevitably interpretative.

Marcel warns that "we must carefully avoid all confusion between the mysterious and the unknowable," and insists that "the recognition of mystery . . . is an essentially positive act of the mind" (BH 118). By "the mysterious," or the metaproblematic, he means the realm where the intelligibility of what is to be understood necessarily involves participant experience. The traditional puzzle about mind and body, for example, must include, in determining its intelligibility, the experience of one who is embodied. An account of society must include reference to the lived experiences of its members, who belong to it as a shared form of life. But, as noted, all expressions of lived experience involve interpretation and a rejection of translation into the "impersonal." Despite Marcel's declared recognition of the metaproblematic as "an essentially positive act of the mind," as sympathetic a critic as Paul Ricoeur has serious reservations regarding the positive use of secondary reflection in Marcel's writings. Ricoeur thinks that Marcel's attack on primary reflection in the form of objectivism, instrumentalism, and so forth has obsessed him to the point of failing to rehabilitate a healthier form of reason: "Without denying," Ricoeur writes, "that this is indeed the present condition of reason, I do not see how one can understand the ontological affirmation without at the same time undertaking a deliverance of reason from its scientifico-technological abasement."[2] In Ricoeur's estimation, Marcel's failure to develop a theory of rationality moves him in the direction of mysticism. Without denying that much of Marcel's work is given over to criticism of the dangers of objectivism, technocracy, and the false universalism of impersonal thinking, there are areas of his project which clearly show a positive side to secondary reflection, for example, drama and narrative. In the latter case, it is worth noting that Marcel was exploring narrative as a form of rationality well before his friend Ricoeur.

"I am convinced," Marcel says in a typical passage, "that it is in drama and through drama that metaphysical thought grasps and defines itself *in concreto*" (PE 26). Action, he thought, was most appropriately understood in the dramatic mode, rather than in "the abstract relationships of inherence or exteriority between which traditional philosophies claimed to make me choose" (PE 126). Drama offers a mode of developing and communicating meaning by a concrete showing. One recalls in this regard the quotation from E. M. Forster with which Marcel introduced the second part of his *Metaphysical Journal* and, as well, his essay "Creative Fidelity": "It is private life that holds out the mirror to infinity" (CF 147). The mirroring in question here, the mirroring that is a showing, is not that which is the target of Richard Rorty's well-known *Philosophy and the Mirror of Nature,* where mirroring is equivalent to reflecting a true picture of an original. Marcel's use of "mirror" is rather that which Ricoeur articulates so well in his writings on *mimesis* as representation: "Far from producing a weakened image of preexisting things, *mimesis* brings about an augmentation of meaning in the field of action, which is its privileged field. It does not equate itself with something already given. Rather it produces what it imitates, if we continue to translate *mimesis* by 'imitation.' "[3] There are echoes of this very usage when Marcel speaks of his own dramatic writing in his essay "The Drama of the Soul in Exile." He places the origins of his plays in certain "seeds" of experience: the dramatic work is "the return of something lent him [the dramatist] to be transmuted . . . if you will, like an outbreathing in which the vital, having been transmuted into the spiritual, again becomes vital, with the spiritualized vitality of dramatic creation" (DSE 22). He likens the transmuting of the vital into the meaningful to "an imaginative activity in some ways comparable to the swarm of hypotheses generated in the scientific mind by an unusual phenomenon" (DSE 23). The dramatist mediates between the vital and the meaningful through his or her creative, imaginative work, producing a "framework" in which the vital takes on meaning. The play is not a copy, but a presentation or work. As a dramatic work, the play is a form of objectification which avoids the decontextualization that defines objectification in its problematic sense. The play demands the work of recontextualization or participatory translation (application) by the audience back into the vital for its referenced meaning. It is for this reason that Marcel insists that in drama "intelligence and sympathy are inextricably mixed." The imaginative, constructive dimension of drama is balanced, in Marcel's remarks, by reference to the vital roots of drama. Just as the framework of a hypothesis can, in its own way, illuminate previously inchoate data, so, in regard to our lives, "the theatre [is] perhaps the best of all vehicles for the truths of illumination . . . for those sudden flashes which now and then light up the vast and undulating landscape of our lives, a landscape through which we may have travelled for years, seeing no more than a yard or two ahead, but whose vistas at such moments take instant shape before our inner eye" (DSE 27–28). Participant experience, as it takes on meaning through a constructive reflection, serves as "guide" for the constructions, allowing a judgment regarding their power of illumination.

In the chapter entitled "My Life" in the first volume of *The Mystery of Being,* Marcel takes up the question of self-knowledge. He rejects the idea of "an objectively valid answer" to the question "Who am I?" With regard to knowing itself, the self is unable to desituate itself, to assume the role of "pure subject" vis-à-vis itself. Marcel draws an analogy between recollecting one's life and making artistic judgments:

> Everything seems to indicate that it would be risky to the last degree to seek, in the judgments of men at some given time, for the definitive and irrevocable: for our appreciations of a work of art are always, say what we will to the contrary, affected by the "climate of the age," they reflect our unconscious assumptions which we share with our contemporaries during some given period of history; the historically conditioned attitude is something which, for all of us, is quite inescapable; and perhaps we cannot even imagine, without tangling ourselves in contradictions, a *dehistoricized* attitude in the name of which completely objective judgments, judgments quite untainted by the local, the temporal, the personal, and in a word quite free from relativity, could be made about works of art, literature, and philosophy. (MB 196–97)

Understanding one's life, then, involves mediation and construction, a historically conditioned reflection. It is here that Marcel introduces the need for narrative: "My life presents itself to reflection as something whose essential nature is that it can be related as a story . . . and this is so very true that one may be permitted to wonder whether the words 'my life' retain any precise meaning at all, if we abstract from the meaning we attach to them any reference whatsoever to the act of narration" (MB 190). The relation of narrative to life is not representational in the usual sense; narrative is not a copy, since as Marcel insists, "it is impossible . . . for me to tell the story of my life just as I have lived it."

One does not "mirror oneself" (in the traditional representational sense) in narrative. Narrative presents life "as a sequence of episodes along the line of time," but the sequence presented is "selective" and is a "summary," not a documentary "reproduction." "Imagination" enters into the constructive dimension of narrative in the putting into shape of life events in terms of meaningful episodes. The constructivist dimension ("a fresh construction of an old site") recognizes that "my life, as it has been really lived, falls outside my thinking's present grasp" (MB 191). Narrative, however, is not sheer construction, imposed willy-nilly upon the pure immediacy of life, because, Marcel tells us, narrative makes "*allusion* to something which, of its very nature, will not let itself be fully expressed in words, and which is something I have lived through." Narrative can awaken "an echo, set certain strings vibrating" by a "luminous flash" (MB 193).

Drama and narrative exhibit the realistic dimension of secondary reflection, which is a "tributary" of one's participation in Being as well as its constructivist dimension of "imaging" indirectly that involvement. Marcel had some regrets about adopting the term "intuition," as is clear from the exchanges he had with the Thomist Jacques Maritain over the notion. Maritain admitted a heavily intellectualist intuition of Being, which Marcel rejected:

> I felt I had to keep asking the same question: "If this intuition of being exists, how is it that so many minds are completely unaware of it?" I myself admit that when someone speaks of an intuition of being, the words signify nothing whatever for me, strictly speaking. At most I might acknowledge today, as I have explicitly done in *Being and Having,* a blinded or blocked intuition. But I think it is debatable whether intuition is even the right word to use for that. (TWB 45–46)

He is aware of being captive to discourse that he is trying to overcome, and "intuition" smacks too much of a certain hubris on the part of the philosopher to have laid hold of Being, encouraging all too easily "the idea of totality." For Marcel, the emphasis is upon the qualification "blinded," a blocking of cognition until mediated by expression. And there is no question of an absorption of blinded intuition by cognitive expression, which, for example, as we have observed in the form of narrative, makes "*allusion*" to a lived experience "which, of its very nature, will not let itself be fully expressed in words." It is crucial to keep this in mind in the light of Marcel's references to reflection as "recovery," which can give the impression of reflection as the quest of return to an original. Perhaps it is in Marcel's frequent valorization of creativity that we can best see his distance from nostalgia: "As soon as there is creation, in whatever degree, we are in the realm of being," for "Being is the principle of inexhaustibility" (BH 150, 102). "Recovery" is not a question of going back to an original. Lived experience is brought to expression in indirect forms that can be reacted to, interpreted, communicated, and reinterpreted. And it is on this level that meaning (rationality) and ethics intertwine.

Art is Marcel's constant model for the coming to meaning of lived experience. Being, which is lived as a concrete, historical situation, comes to thematization in "structures constituted through what we call the creative process, which offer themselves to the appreciation not only of the subject, in this case the artist, but also of other possible viewers or listeners" (TWB 5). In essays in *Tragic Wisdom and Beyond,* Marcel retrieves the notion of "structure" which he employed in his Gifford Lectures, the two volumes of *The Mystery of Being.* In the latter, he referred to structure as "an intelligible background" against which human intercourse takes place, a background which is not itself an object for its participants. The structure, lived by its participants, serves as a "light" in making sense of phenomena: "It is a necessary condition of all appresentation that the appresenting being should be placed in the middle of a light that will allow something to appear to that being, to be made manifest to it" (TWB 87). Phenomena, data, and "facts" are not meaningful in themselves, and appear so only in the light of "structures": "Facts have no existence or power that is intrinsic to themselves. . . . [W]hat I have called 'fact' can be regarded as a property of our postulated structure; it is in some sense integrated into the structure, and it is for this reason that it can become radiant" (MB 83). Facts will become "radiant," that is, make sense, in terms of a background that can illuminate them. But, as well, the background must in some way "fit" the facts, so that structures do not simply impose themselves brutally on facts. The distinction between activity and passivity breaks down in considering the relationship between facts and structures: "Let us say in a very general way that at this level the contrast between activity and passivity—between activity, say, considered as taking, and reception considered as being given something—loses a great deal of its meaning; in the dimension in which we now find ourselves, we must move beyond such categories" (MB 83). In his essay "What Can Be Expected of Philosophy?" he claims that "it is only on the basis of structure, whatever it might be, that the intersubjective communion can be established" (TWB 5), and in "Authentic Humanism," that "existential assurance relates to the structural conditions that allow an individual to open himself to others" (TWB 38). One can see here a suggestion of public or instituted forms which mediate all communication, something like Merleau-Ponty's notion of the *intermonde*. This is a welcome recognition of a notion of objectification that is not pejorative, but it remains, unfortunately, undeveloped.

Marcel, of course, is noted for the central place in his thinking occupied by the I/Thou relationship. The dialogical "I" is decentered in its welcoming openness to and disposition to listen to the Other. Dialogue implies respect for an Other that transcends categories of having, instrumentality, reduction, objectivity, such that I experience in dialogue the "hold" that the Other has over me. In the course of his writings, Marcel displays the dialogical relation as a contrast to various forms of objectivism, but in *Tragic Wisdom and Beyond* it appears embedded in terms of a communicative rationality in discussions of philosophy and art (poetry and music), the "structural" conditions of which Marcel now brings out. Creative expression takes place through given structures, which are taken up and shaped by an existential meaning, as when in the case of a piece of music we become aware of "a certain quality made present to us through the structure, a certain sadness" (TWB 5). Having introduced the notion of structure, Marcel fumbles to clarify. He is not, he protests, committing himself to "formalism." Structures as given modes of communication must not be confused with the "communion" of shared meaning. The public structures are not themselves existential universals, that is, meanings which take subjects into account. It is only in the phenomena of expression themselves and not on the level of the blinded intuition that one might speak of a "universality."

And it is, once again, to art that Marcel turns for his examples: "In art subjectivity tends to pass over into an intersubjectivity which is entirely different from the objectivity science honors so much, but which nonetheless completely surpasses the limits of the individual consciousness taken in isolation" (TWB 6). As long as there is lived experience and expression, the universal is an open process, a task rather than an achievement. Philosophy is thought in analogy with art: "Philosophical experience requires a living communication with other experiences *already elaborated,* that is, dialogue with other philosophers" (TWB 9; emphasis added). Marcel regards as "negligible" any "philosophical experience that is not able to welcome an experience other than itself" (TWB 7). I emphasize the element of elaboration, which makes clear the public, structural, instituted dimension of philosophy which calls for interpretation and dialogue with Others. Art and philosophy are forms of communicative rationality, what Marcel calls "fraternal comprehension," operating by exchanges of a dialogical nature which imply "mutual comprehension and respect for each other" (TWB 30). "Fraternal comprehension" does not require unanimity. Marcel ends his preface to *Tragic Wisdom and Beyond* with a dedication to Nietzsche: "It is in the spirit of Nietzsche that the following reflections are offered" (TWB xxxv). In many ways Marcel and Nietzsche are flatly opposed, but as Marcel notes, "it is essential that philosophical experience, once it is explicitly worked out, confront other experiences which are themselves elaborated. . . . One could go further, and say that this confrontation itself is actually part of the experience" (TWB 8).

In the early part of the twentieth century, Marcel concluded that the mainstream movements of modern philosophy had played themselves out and that new approaches were called for. He rejected, in particular, "the abstract relationships of inherence or exteriority between which traditional philosophies claimed to make me choose." As he struggled to find his own voice, he realized and honestly faced the fact that the discrediting of modern thought constituted a crisis of thought itself. This situation prompted him to contribute to a refiguration of philosophy whose centerpiece would be thinking in the form of secondary reflection. I have argued, on the basis of his treatment of drama and narrative, that secondary reflection is interpretation and that his late essays demonstrate a communicative rationality in the context of which his ethical I/Thou relationship takes on social and historical flesh. I believe a major factor in Marcel's philosophical development in this regard was his continuous preoccupation with art. He told Ricoeur: "The truth is that the connection between philosophy and drama in my case is the closest, the most intimate possible" (TWB 230). Indeed, whenever pressed to define basic philosophical categories—truth, self, thought, universality—he turned to art for his analogies. Marcel appreciated, as one of the central aspects of art, creativity. Speaking of art and philosophy to Ricoeur, he said: "Actually, what strikes me now after so many years is that I still find in my plays a kind of living interest or freshness which seems to be somewhat lacking in my philosophical writings to the extent that they are in some way too explicit, too summary, or have occasioned too many commentaries which are often mere repetitions rather than creative reflections" (TWB 236). Actually, the course of philosophy has turned very much in the direction taken by Marcel. Emphasis upon embodiment, his decentering and socializing of the subject, his deliberate undermining of systematization, his critique of instrumental rationality, his incipient views of interpretation and communicative rationality—these are mainstream notions today. When I read Marcel thirty years ago, colleagues dismissed him to me as "too effeminate," meaning, I presume, that he lacked logical rigor, was sensitive to relationships, embodied the subject, criticized technology, emphasized dialogue. Yet I have not read one feminist who has found resonances with his work, while many have with Nietzsche. Surely, Marcel was in many ways patriarchal. So was Nietzsche. Today, instead of Marcel's being recognized as a thinker who helped to bring us into the postmodern world, his works are allowed to fall out of print. Many who read Marcel in another, essentialist, direction from my own would, I think, just as well suffer his works to drop from print as to see him read in terms of postmodernism. Admittedly, I ask of Marcel's texts questions of attention today, but it was, after all, Marcel himself who desired that his philosophical works be read with creative reflection rather than repetitious commentary. I hope to have established that his works yield much, without being forced, in the line of a developing hermeneutics and communicative rationality.

He clearly rejected the "definitive and irrevocable" for the "historically conditioned attitude . . . which, for all of us, is quite inescapable." "Works of art, literature, and philosophy" are never "untainted by the local, the temporal, the personal, and in a word quite free from relativity." If, as I have argued, the work of art served as his exemplar of understanding, then I think it clear that, for Marcel, one never gets beyond interpretation.

> The work of art is there for us to contemplate and, in a certain sense, for us to draw life from; but if we do draw more life from it, that is only by virtue of the act by which, opening ourselves to it and interpreting it for ourselves, we make it our own. For one's interpretation of a work of art is related fairly strictly to the sort of person one is, and therefore, in the case of every significant work of art, there is a wide and varied range of possible interpretations. It would be quite an illusion to imagine that there is a kind of nucleus which subsists independently of, and which is unamenable to, all interpretation. (MB 195–96)

This is not to deny that thought is "the pursuit of the Other," but rather is to affirm that all approaches to Being are indirect, are elaborations. It is precisely in the elaborated circulation of Being, in its exchanges across perspectives, that is experienced the call to fraternity.

## WORKS OF MARCEL CITED

BH    *Being and Having.* Trans. Kathleen Farrer. New York: Harper, 1965 (*Être et avoir.* Paris: Aubier, 1935).

CF    *Creative Fidelity.* Trans. Robert Rosthal. New York: Noonday, 1964 (*Du Refus à l'invocation.* Paris: Gallimard, 1940).

DSE   *"The Drama of the Soul in Exile."* Trans. Rosalind Heywood. In *Gabriel Marcel: Three Plays,* 13–34. New York: Hill and Wang, 1965.

MB    *The Mystery of Being.* Vol. 1, *Reflection and Mystery.* Trans. G. S. Fraser. Chicago: Regnery, 1960 (*Le Mystère de l'être.* Vol. 1. Paris: Aubier, 1952).

MJ    *Metaphysical Journal.* Trans. Bernard Wall. Chicago: Regnery, 1952 (*Journal métaphysique.* Paris: Gallimard, 1927).

MM    *Man Against Mass Society.* Trans. G. S. Fraser. Chicago: Regnery, 1962 (*Les Hommes contre l'humain.* Paris: La Colombe, 1951).

PE    *The Philosophy of Existentialism.* Trans. Manya Harari. New York: Philosophical Library, 1969 (contains "On the Ontological Mystery" and "An Essay in Autobiography") (*Position et approches concrètes du mystère ontologique.* Paris: Vrin, 1949).

TWB   *Tragic Wisdom and Beyond.* Trans. Stephen Jolin and Peter McCormick. Evanston, Ill.: Northwestern University Press, 1973 (*Pour une sagesse tragique et au-delà.* Paris: Plon, 1968).

## NOTES

1. "Reply to Pietro Prini," in *The Philosophy of Gabriel Marcel,* ed. Paul Schilpp and Lewis Hahn (LaSalle, Ill.: Open Court, 1984), 240.

2. Paul Ricoeur, "Gabriel Marcel and Phenomenology," ibid., 490.

3. Paul Ricoeur, "Mimesis and Representation," in *Reflection and Imagination: A Ricoeur Reader,* ed. Mario Valdes (Toronto: University of Toronto Press, 1991), 138.

## WORKS CONSULTED

*Bulletin de la Société Americaine de la Philosophie de Langue Française.* Special issue on Marcel. Spring 1995.

Cooney, William, ed. *Contributions of Gabriel Marcel to Philosophy.* Lewiston, N.Y.: Edwin Mellon, 1989.

Schilpp, Paul, and Lewis Hahn, eds. *The Philosophy of Gabriel Marcel.* LaSalle, Ill.: Open Court, 1984.

Valdes, Mario, ed. *Reflection and Imagination: A Ricoeur Reader.* Toronto: University of Toronto Press, 1991.

# 3

# Jean-Paul Sartre and Judith Butler: Phenomenological and Poststructuralist Existentialism

SEVERAL YEARS AGO, I included Judith Butler's *Gender Trouble* in a course on subjectivity and identity. In fact, I substituted her book for Foucault's *Discipline and Punishment*, which I had been using in conjunction with selections from Sartre and Ricoeur, since I considered Butler's work to be a brilliant adaptation of Foucault's notion of the production of subjectivity to issues of gender. As my students and I read and discussed *Gender Trouble*, I found to my surprise that along with the expected resonances with Foucault that I planned to feature, strong resonances with Sartre began to emerge as well. This impression grew with each rereading of *Gender Trouble*, as I came to judge that the most interesting and novel aspect of the book was not the discourse of production but rather the discourse of "repetition" and "resignification." The latter reminded me of Sartre's *Saint Genet: Actor and Martyr*, the work that Sartre claimed to have come the closest to expressing his understanding of freedom: "What is important is not what people make of us, but what we ourselves make of what others have made of us" (SG 60). Sartre here acknowledges a discourse of production ("what others have made of us") as well as a discourse of transformation ("what we make of what others have made of us"). The scant references to Sartre in *Gender Trouble* are all very negative. He is dismissed as a phallocentric and dualistic thinker, while all credit for breaking with the metaphysics of identity goes to Nietzsche. It was only after reading *Gender Trouble* that I read Butler's first book, *Subjects of Desire,* two chapters of which deal with Sartre's philosophy.

In *Subjects of Desire,* Butler organizes her treatment of Sartre around her thematic of imagination and desire. She traces out the development of these themes and their entanglement in his ontology, which has deep roots in the *cogito* tradition. Then, in a very sensitive and intelligent shift, she looks at how imagination and desire appear in Sartre's psychobiographies of Genet and Flaubert. She notes that the "earlier ontological schematism is historicized through his biographical inquiries" (SD 167). In particular, being-for-itself, which appeared on the scene in *Being and Nothingness* as a given subjectivity—alert, active, constituting meaning, and undoubtedly masculine—appears in the biographies as an infant—vulnerable, dependent, and subject to social interpellations. Butler recognizes the significance of the reconceptualization of the ontological categories as they are employed as working tools in the biographies. When she writes that "Sartre understands subjectivity not only as the culmination of a history of circumstances but, more importantly, as the singular realization or determination of this history" (SD 164), Butler is sensitive to the new understanding of situatedness and freedom revealed in the biographies. In *Being and Nothingness,* all too often Sartre opposed freedom and situatedness in subject/object fashion, preserving the free subject from determination by distancing it from being submerged into its situation. This is why Sartre took up the *cogito* tradition, since it guaranteed, as it were, a subject at a distance from its objects. It is just this ontological understanding of the subject which is being rethought as it is being "applied" in the biographies. With regard to Genet, Butler notes that "Sartre's biography of Genet traces a career that begins with victimization and culminates in radical invention" (SD 159). But the "radical invention" is not understood as an invention *ex nihilo,* for as Butler observes, "[Genet's] tools are wrought from the weapons originally turned against him; he becomes the master of inversion" (SD 160). This impressed me with its similarity to Butler's own version of agency and, in particular, parodic inversion in *Gender Trouble* and served to provoke me to think more about resonances and differences with regard to identity, body, subjectivity, and psychoanalysis in the work of Sartre and Butler.

In Sartre's *The Flies,* Orestes, the existentialist protagonist, proclaims that "justice is a matter between men" (F 103). He makes this claim against the two authoritative orders of religion and politics, represented by Zeus and Aegistheus, respectively. The latter claims a birthright to rule, while the former justifies himself as well by appeal to the "natural order." In a climactic and somewhat comedic scene, Zeus and Orestes square off. Against a backdrop of "the firmament, spangled with wheeling stars," with an amplified voice, Zeus attempts to situate Orestes in the natural order, to put him in his place. Zeus identifies himself as the author of the natural order, points out its cosmological ("Hear the music of the spheres . . .") and biological ("man shall beget man, and dog give birth to dog . . .") dimensions, and then commands Orestes: "Return to nature, Nature's thankless son . . . you are a mite in the scheme of things" (F 117). In a rejoinder that utterly deflates Zeus, Orestes exclaims: "Outside nature, against nature, without excuse, beyond remedy, except what remedy I find within myself" (F 119). Orestes assumes a place "on the far side of despair," without the comforts of a founded space, a new space where he, and others, must invent themselves and their justice. The rather overblown drama exemplifies Sartre's project of rethinking identity which began in *The Transcendence of the Ego* (1936), where he explicitly linked this rethinking with a new approach to ethics and politics. The concluding sentence of *The Transcendence of the Ego* is: "No more is needed in the way of a philosophical foundation for an ethics and a politics which are absolutely positive" (TE 106). While often seriously wrongheaded about political issues, Sartre was doggedly consistent in his defense of the oppressed as he spoke out effectively against colonialism, racism, and classism. In the philosophical analysis supporting his politics, he continued to see the issue of identity at the heart of justifications for oppression.

For thinking about identity, Sartre adopted a dangerous tool: Husserl's phenomenology. It offered him the language of reduction and constitution, a way of making the givenness of identity tremble and of revealing what was originally taken as a given to be a constituted product. Yet, Husserl's phenomenology was tied to the tradition of the *cogito,* to a version of subjectivity that tended to undermine Sartre's very deep commitment to situatedness. Indeed, one can say that it is the tension or play of subjectivity and situatedness that is at the heart of all of Sartre's philosophical thinking, which at various times privileges one over the other as he tries to think them together. At his best in *Being and Nothingness,* Sartre maintains the ambiguous tension between "transcendence" and "facticity" expressed in "I am not what I am and am what I am not," a way of articulating that one is never a free subjectivity beyond or outside of the obligation to sustain an identity ("It would be absurd even to think of existing otherwise than in a situation," BN 526), while the identity is never closure ("The principle of identity, far from being a universal axiom universally applied, is only a synthetic principle enjoying a merely regional universality," BN 58). At his worst, and during those occasions when he stresses his opposition to the determinism of closure, he will stress the subjectivity of the *cogito,* a wholly active subjectivity beyond the reach of its situation ("For human reality, to be is to *choose oneself;* nothing comes to it from the outside or from within which it can *receive or accept,*" BN 440).

From his beginning in *The Transcendence of the Ego,* Sartre clearly rejects naturalistic and other forms of essentialistic foundationalism in thinking about identity. For Sartre, essentialism takes the result of actions as their cause: "*Really,* consciousnesses are first; through these are constituted states; and then, through the latter, the ego is constituted. But, as the order is reversed by a consciousness which imprisons itself in the world in order to flee from itself, consciousnesses are given as emanating from states, and states as produced by the ego" (TE 81). The ego, as a fixed form of identity, is a product of a certain wrongheaded way of thinking about ourselves. Actually, Sartre argues in *The Transcendence of the Ego,* the ego is constituted by a radically free consciousness. In *Being and Nothingness* (1943), Sartre identifies radically free consciousness as being-for-itself, a mode of being that does not "coincide" with itself. The lack of coincidence is due to a form of self-consciousness that is a dimension of every act of consciousness. In being intentionally aware of an object, consciousness is at the same time tacitly aware of itself. This has the effect of "splitting" consciousness from identity with itself, compelling it to exist as "presence to itself." The difference within itself which precludes self-identity is called by Sartre *néant.* Sartre is a philosopher of difference, as one refers to that term today, but his is a psychological rather than linguistic sense of difference. The result of difference is that deep identity is impossible to human reality. His way of expressing this ontologically is somewhat awkward: "Human reality [is] a being which *is* what it is not and which *is not* what it is" (BN 58). To say that one "is not what one is" is to say that one never is anything in the mode of deep identity. To say that one "is what one is not" is to say that one is not a freedom/subjectivity outside of identity, but that one exists at, or sustains, one's identity. For Sartre, one of the outcomes of the split of the self from identity with itself is its temporality. Temporality disperses or defers deep identity, with the result that "making replaces being" (BN 62). "Being" is an "ideal" or "regulative meaning" (BN 61), even a "social demand" or "obligation" (BN 59). However, there is inevitable "failure" to be in the deep sense, because of the ontological structure of being-for-itself. The *néant*, or difference, splitting the being of consciousness from itself creates an inevitable excess or remainder on the "outside" of identity. A person *is* his or her actions, but *not* wholly so: "The *self* therefore represents an ideal distance within the immanence of the subject in relation to himself, a way of *not being his own coincidence,* of escaping identity while positing it as unity—in short, of being in a perpetually unstable equilibrium between identity as absolute cohesion without a trace of diversity, and unity as a synthesis of multiplicity" (BN 77). This "perpetually unstable equilibrium" is the basis of Sartre's own use of "trouble" with respect to identity. For him all identity is "troubled." "Thus, by the sole fact that my belief is apprehended [tacitly] as belief, it *is no longer only belief;* that is, it is already no longer belief, it is troubled [*troublée*] belief" (BN 74–75).

These "best" and "worst" faces of Sartre wrestle with one another throughout *Being and Nothingness.* More often than not, the worst face prevails. An example of this, one which will help bring Sartre's views into comparison with Butler's, is the brief discussion of social reality and exigency tucked away in the section "My Fellowman." "To live in a world haunted by my fellowman," Sartre writes, "means . . . that in the midst of a world already provided with meaning I meet with a meaning which is *mine* and which I have not given to myself, which I discover that I 'possess already' " (BN 510). Among these meanings are nationality, race, and physical appearance, as well as the exigencies of the "instrumental complexes" of the world (laws, machines, techniques in general). The social world consists of so many "imperatives," "directions furnished by others." Social imperatives and techniques, however, do not bring about deep identity. One must "exist" as a Frenchman or as a worker. Existence supposes a certain taking on or "know-how" about French or worker identities. Social identities and exigencies do not take away human freedom: "The for-itself can choose itself only beyond certain meanings of which it is not the origin. Each for-itself, in fact, is a for-itself only by choosing itself beyond nationality and race just as it speaks only by choosing the designation beyond the syntax and morphemes. This 'beyond' is enough to assure its total independence in relation to the structures which it surpasses" (BN 520). The use of "beyond" and "total independence" with regard to social structures points to the danger with appropriating Husserl's philosophical discourse, which can perhaps be seen here in the suggestion of a subject confronting social structures as objects. It is a question of understanding what Sartre means by "transcendence," or freedom in regard to social structures. At times he appears to indicate that the *néant,* or break in being constitutive of freedom, is sharp and clean to the point of detachment: "But if consciousness exists in terms of the given, this does not mean that the given conditions consciousness; consciousness is a pure and simple negation of the given" (BN 478). At other times, in the language of "am and am not" ("I am and am not a Frenchman") the "am not" is not so clean and suggestive of detachment, for it is bound to and balanced by the "am."

The same problem is apparent in Sartre's treatment of the body in his ontology. He insists that subjectivity (being-for-itself) is body: "The body is nothing other than the for-itself"; "Being-for-itself must be wholly body and it must be wholly consciousness; it can not be *united* with a body. There is nothing *behind* the body" (BN 309, 305). To be a body is to be situated: "The body is not distinct from the *situation* of the for-itself since for the for-itself, to exist and to be situated are one and the same"; "To say that I have entered into the world . . . or that there is a world, or that I have a body is one and the same thing" (BN 309, 318). But, for Sartre, to be in the world is not the same as to be *in the midst* of the world as mere things are. Thus, the human body is not a pure thing, but rather the site of the break with the identity of things: "I *am* my body to the extent that I *am; I am not* my body to the extent that I am not what I am. It is by my nihilation that I escape it. . . . The body is necessary . . . as the obstacle to be surpassed in order to be in the world" (BN 326). Sartre can be his own worst enemy, opening himself here to his critics' (including Butler's) charge that he recapitulates Cartesian dualism and Western phallocentric metaphysics. The sense of "am not" is embedded in a discourse of surpassing, escape, and obstacle, which readily yields to such criticism. However, other aspects of his discussion complicate the issue and put in question this sort of interpretation. The sense of surpassing and escape, for example, can be read more generously. Sartre uses the example of pain. For him, the body "exists its pain—i.e., itself—as a wrenching away from self. Pure pain as the simple 'lived' can not be reached; it belongs to the category of indefinables and indescribables which are what they are. . . . [P]ain as a contingent attachment to the world can be existed non-thetically by consciousness only if it is surpassed" (BN 333). I take him to mean that the human body is the site where the "purely" physical breaks up, is differenced. Pure physical pain is always the "past" which is surpassed. But the surpassing does not exit the physical, leave it behind for the nonphysical. Rather, pain is existed (surpassed, escaped) "as" the punishment of the gods, intolerable, bearable, a test of character, the evidence of the meaninglessness of life, and so forth. Sartre does not deny the physicality of the human body. His claim is that the factical physical's closure in terms of pure states breaks up. The physical can be reached only as it is understood through the ways in which it is broken up in surpassings: "It is impossible to grasp facticity in its brute nudity, since all that we will find of it is already recovered and freely constructed" (BN 83). The body, for Sartre, is a "meaningful" phenomenon, and therefore is social and cultural.

A politics of the body must today pass through the work of Judith Butler, whose aim is to "trouble" both gender as a stable identity and the very notion of identity itself to disclose "the political stakes" that are consequent: "We ought to ask what political possibilities are the consequence of a radical critique of the categories of identity" (GT xi). Butler begins by questioning a

prevalent assumption of feminist theory, "that there is some existing identity, understood through the category of women" (GT
1), in terms of which "women's" interests might be represented.
For Butler, there is no preexisting political subject to be represented by such a "juridical" or "foundationalist" politics. Following Foucault's lead, Butler rejects universals and general
ontological principles in favor of historical/genealogical investigations. Feminists who would themselves appeal to universals and
general ontological principles are evidence that "the colonizing
gesture is not primarily or irreducibly masculine" (GT 13). The
feminist undermining of patriarchal essentialism must result in the
repudiation of all essentialism. She is, as well, suspicious of "dialogical" or "coalitional" politics, which, because of its naïveté
regarding "the power relations that condition and limit dialogical
possibilities" (GT 15), tends to set up in advance an ideal outcome which would steer all dialogue. Instead of a politics which
would assume an initial existing foundation or an ideal future one,
based on identity, Butler employs Foucault to establish her claim
that "juridical systems of power *produce* the subjects they subsequently come to represent" (GT 15). These structures produce
and define subjects through prohibition and control (including
even the according of rights). The first political task, then, is to
create genealogies of power, which are hidden behind stable identities, in order to reveal the contingency of identity.

After "troubling" the identity of women, Butler moves on to
trouble the identity of "sex." She notes that most people today
are inclined to see "gender" as a social production and "sex" as a
pre-given biological surface on which gender comes to be inscribed. But if there can be multiple understandings of gender, it
seems to follow that sex does not cause gender in a determining
sense. But why, Butler asks, assume "sex" to be a naturally given
foundation for inscription? Does not sex have a "history"? Is it
not actually the product of medico-juridical discourses? Her suggestion: "Gender is not to culture as sex is to nature; gender is
also the discursive/cultural means by which 'sexed nature' or 'a
natural sex' is produced and established as 'prediscursive,' prior to
culture" (GT 7). One thinks sex through gender. What Butler
says of sex, of course, translates as well to "body." All real bodies
are differenced. "But 'the body' is itself a construction, as are the

myriad 'bodies' that constitute the domain of gendered subjects. Bodies cannot be said to have a signifiable existence prior to the mark of their gender" (GT 8). Butler's constructivism has been the target of several critics for being a form of idealism or denial of physical existence and occasioned a response/clarification in *Bodies That Matter*. Here she points out that "materiality" and "sex" are both notions with a history, which is not to deny that these notions refer:

> To "concede" the undeniability of "sex" or its "materiality" is always to concede some version of "sex," some formation of "materiality." Is the discourse in and through which that concession occurs—and, yes, that concession invariably does occur—not itself formative of the very phenomenon that it concedes? To claim that discourse is formative is not to claim that it originates, causes, or exhaustively composes that which it concedes; rather, it is to claim that there is no reference to a pure body which is not at the same time a further formation of that body. (BTM 10)

While the body is not "simply linguistic stuff," "it bears on language all the time." Butler borrows from Merleau-Ponty to clarify her position when she writes: "Language and materiality are fully embedded in each other, chiasmic in their interdependency, but never fully collapsed into one another, i.e., reduced to one another, and yet neither fully ever exceeds the other. . . . [L]anguage and materiality are never fully identical nor fully different" (BTM 69). Language "materializes" matter, forming its intelligibility. One cannot compare materialization to matter, but only various materializations to one another. In this way, Butler speaks of the function of "interpellations" in materializing sexed bodies and social identities in general. "It's a girl!" is not a description, but a prescription, or rather a "performative": "You will be a girl." Gender/sex is "an ideal construct which is forcibly materialized through time." For Butler (as for Sartre), deep identity is always a failure: "Bodies never quite comply with the norms by which their materialization is impelled" (BTM 2), and " 'being' a sex or a gender is fundamentally impossible" (GT 19). Discourse can produce effects only through "reiterative and citational practices," so that the effects are never finally realized. As soon as Butler establishes her point that gender/sex is socially produced, she emphasizes its instability and transformability. The reiterative and citational practices that sustain identity are the very means of its subversion and reworking. Identity is "open to intervention and resignification" (GT 33). It is in this context that Butler introduces her understanding of subjectivity/agency.

"To claim that the subject is itself produced in and as a gendered matrix of relations is not to do away with the subject, but only to ask after the conditions of its emergence and operation" (BTM 7). Butler's elaboration of the subject steers a course between a determinism which would make "a mockery of human agency" and "the voluntarist subject of humanism." Consistent with her rejection of the prediscursive, Butler opts for a culturally formed subject: "Construction is not opposed to agency; it is the necessary scene of agency" (GT 11). In being produced, the subject is limited insofar as it is formed by a particular discursive matrix of possibilities. Yet, at the same time, it is enabled by those very possibilities, which can serve as the reworking of the original matrix: "To be *implicated* in the relations of power, indeed enabled by the relations of power that the 'I' opposes is not, as a consequence, to be reducible to their existing forms" (BTM 123). This irreducibility is displayed in Butler's well-known example of gender "parody" through drag, where the productive reiteration of norms is revealed through a variation of their citation. Here it is evident that subjectivity does not step out of its implication in gender/identity to subvert it, but utilizes its own produced/productive resources to resignify itself, to challenge the very "law" that produces it.

Butler separates her understanding of subjectivity/agency from that of the existentialists (Sartre, Merleau-Ponty, de Beauvoir), whom she accuses of harboring "a pre-discursive structure for both the self and its acts" (GT 8). With the prediscursive self comes a dualism between self and body, self and language, self and institutions. The existentialists' use of the term "embodiment" is suspicious for Butler, carrying as it does "theological contexts" (the Incarnation) and thus preserving "the external and dualistic relationship between a signifying immateriality and the materiality of the body itself" (GT 152 n. 15). As we have noted, there is a way in which Sartre thinks of subjectivity that is heavily laced with a *cogito* discourse, justifying suspicions such as Butler's. Yet there are other of his articulations of subject and identity which seem indistinguishable from hers. Her own views would appear to establish that I both am and am not my gender. Both Sartre and Butler reject essentialism and the metaphysics of substance and agree that "making" replaces "being" with regard to gender. The major difference regards the understanding of "making," for Sartre appears to hold that making is a free project, depending upon choice, while Butler thinks that it is a social imposition, "made" in the form of reiteration of norms. But if we take into consideration Sartre's later work, including the psychobiographies, this very differentiation between Sartre and Butler becomes open to question.

Both Genet and Flaubert are called into being by various interpellations. In the case of Genet, "a voice declares publicly: You're a thief. . . . It is revealed to [the child] that he *is* a thief and he pleads guilty, crushed by a fallacy which he is unable to refute. . . . [He] is provided with a monstrous and guilty ego" (SG 26– 27). Already Genet had been interpellated at birth as illegitimate. He felt himself to be signified, "on the side of the objects named." Flaubert, according to Sartre, because of his male anatomy, had been rejected by his mother, who wanted a daughter. His mother's attitude toward him produced in Flaubert a "passive" nature. He was interpellated as well as the "second son" by his father and produced into social, intelligible being with certain professional expectations. These interpellations, it is clear, were constitutive of both men, in the sense that their agency was an empowerment due their production. "In determining himself in his work as the Thief, Genet escapes this determination" (SG 597). In fact, in his writing, wherein Genet reproduces himself as thief, "he is liberating himself from [his identity] by dint of repeating it" (SG 586). The child Genet had no recourse (other than perhaps killing himself) but to live on the terms set by others. Yet those terms can be met only by a sustained repetition, which in Genet's case eventuated in the literary repetition of himself as thief. His writing brought those practices of repetition to his awareness to the point where he could vary them ("parody" them?) and imaginatively reinvent himself. Flaubert, as well, experienced himself "as a signified without being a signifier" (FI 143). Passivity, however, is not a metaphysical state: "passivity *does not simply exist,* it must be continually created" (FI 42). The sense of "created" here is not voluntaristic. Flaubert does not exist as a subject outside of his passivity: "What is taken is what is at hand, limiting means; poles can be fashioned into spears, nothing more. Those pointed weapons, whatever one does with them, will remain pieces of wood, and their linear materiality does not depend on their new function but on the distant operations which produced that function and are preserved within it" (FI 43). The idea of "limiting means" embraces the senses of both limitation and enablement at the center of Butler's understanding of subjectivity/agency. There is clearly no creation *ex nihilo* in the psychobiographies. Nor was this the case with Sartre's analysis of class identity in his *Critique of Dialectical Reason,* in which he features the woman who works in the Dop shampoo factory (an example he borrows from Claude Lanzmann) to display the production of people through class:

> A working woman who earns 25,000 francs a month and contracts chronic eczema by handling Dop shampoo eight hours a day is wholly reduced to her work, her fatigue, her wages and the material impossibilities that these wages assign her: the impossibility of eating properly, of buying shoes, of sending her child to the country, and of satisfying her most modest wishes. Oppression does not reach the oppressed in a particular sector of their life; it constitutes that life in its totality. They are not people plus needs: they are completely reducible to their needs. There is no distance between self and self, no essence is hidden within the bounds of interiority: the person exists outside, in his relations to the world, and visible to all. (CDR 232)

It is not that the woman does not choose (how to apportion her wages, for example), but that her choices are caught up in structures ("a framework of exigencies") that constitute a "destiny." Her actions are a "repetition" and "realization" of the exigencies that define her life. As an economic agent, the woman has no power other than that afforded by her place within the system. Sartre reminds himself: "I used to say that one never *is* a coward or a thief. Accordingly, should I not now say that one *makes oneself* a bourgeois or a proletarian? . . . There can be no doubt that one *makes oneself* a bourgeois. . . . But in order to make oneself bourgeois, one must be bourgeois" (CDR 231). One always already is something in the sense of being socially defined. But social definition is not an internal essence determining one's actions. Social exigencies, norms, and ideals must be lived or made. For this reason, the workings of social phenomena can be disrupted. Workers can use their economic agency in a strike in order to modify conditions of production and their role therein. Sartre stresses in his discussion of the rise of anarcho-syndicalism in the nineteenth century how the rebellious agency of workers was both enabled and limited by their precise circumstances. The particular form of their subversiveness was "the only effective struggle that was possible in *these* circumstances and against *these* employers" (CDR 241).

Despite her sensitive reading of the psychobiographies in reference to the change of direction from Cartesian abstractions toward historical concreteness in Sartre's thought, as well as her admiration for much of de Beauvoir's work, Butler thinks that the phenomenological tradition is too dangerous, that its discourse harbors yet the memory of the Cartesian subject that only traffics with the body, a view of the self which "runs counter to contemporary findings on the linguistic construction of personal agency" (PI 506). However, her turn to the work of Foucault in order to account for the gendered subject revealed its own dangers. Foucault's account did indeed displace the vestiges of Cartesianism, but was perceived to be inadequate to account for resistance and transformation. Thus we observe Butler undertaking "a psychoanalytic criticism of Foucault," a "reformulation of Foucault" (SRR 232). She remains, in this project, faithful to her commitment to the prediscursive. Her claim that the psychic is discursively formed likens her project to that of Lacan, but she hastens to separate herself from what she perceives to be his constructivist determinism. While Lacan views the gendered subject in terms of the symbolic law, the law, as she reads it, remains only subject to imaginary, and thus ineffective, challenge. Lacan fails to appreciate the Derridean insight that the law functions by a repetitional citation that is open to reworking. Because the symbolic law constitutes gendered identity through prohibition, the very "reality" of the subject, in being "normalized," made "coherent," is produced as a repudiation. Recall that production is not a creation *ex nihilo,* but a bringing into significance. The materialization of the body produces a socially intelligible body, but at a cost. The cost is the "remainder" or "outside" which discursive production inevitably implies. This is the body produced as unintelligible, not the sublimated body but the repressed body, the body as a "loss" which destabilizes the socially intelligible body as an "excess" which haunts the production as rejected possibility. The socially intelligible body is thus incomplete and unstable. Thus, while Butler believes that a theory of repression is required to make sense of resistance, she accounts for repression through social constitution, thereby routing the remnants of essentialism from psychoanalysis in favor of discursive production. With Butler's thoroughgoing commitment to the discursive before us, it is now possible to compare her views with those of Sartre.

There are structural similarities between the stories that Sartre and Butler tell about identity. Both "trouble" identity, Sartre by appropriating Husserl's notions of reduction and constitution, Butler by employing Nietzschean/Foucaultian genealogy and Derrida's deconstruction. Each unmasks the myth of naturalism and essentialism to reveal the contingency of identity. Both substitute the process of "making" for the "being" of identity, while claiming that there is inevitable "failure" to achieve complete identity. Both posit a "subject" which, while constituted/produced by social constraint, has sufficient agency to reinvent itself.

The difference between Sartre and Butler is evident in the latter's rejection of consciousness and experience for the discursive. Sartre understands subjectivity in terms of "lived experience" (*le vécu*): "Today, the notion of 'lived experience' represents an effort to preserve that presence to self which seems to me indispensable for the existence of any psychic fact, while at the same time this presence is so opaque and blind before itself that it is also an absence from itself. Lived experience is always simultaneously present to itself and absent from itself" (IT 42). Human conscious life is "presence to self," and this prevents reduction to identity. There is, for Sartre, inevitable "excess," brought about by the difference (*néant*) of consciousness from itself. The "excess" which foils identity is always already in action and language and never exists apart from them, no more than linguistic difference exists apart from a text. Lived experience, then, does not exist behind action or speech. With regard to the former, action is lived experience so that one is and is not one's actional identity. With regard to speech, the later Sartre came to realize that, without being reduced to one another, existence and language overlap and intermingle: "What is fully lived is never untouched by words . . . since the reality of man living and speaking is created from moment to moment by the mingling of these two orders" (FI 28). Sartre came to see how the subject is constituted through various forms of social constraint and how one's capacity to act is developed situationally: "The most individual possible is only the internalization and enrichment of a social possible" (SM 95). Constraint, however, is not determinism. As a failure to be, one's life is always open to transfiguration. Consider Sartre's portrayal of intellectuals as potential revolutionaries in "A Plea for Intellectuals":

> Today, the bourgeois ideology with which the technicians of practical knowledge are initially impregnated by their education in the "humanities," contradicts the other component part of themselves, their function as researchers, equipped with specific knowledges and methods. They are universalist because they seek universal forms of knowledge and practice. But if they apply their methods to an examination of the ruling class and its ideology—which is also *their own*—they cannot hide from themselves the fact that both are surreptitiously particularist. At that moment, in their research, they discover alienation; they become aware that they are the instruments of ends which remain foreign to them and which they are forbidden to question. (PFI 240)

The intellectual, as one who becomes aware of his or her social situation as Sartre depicts it, is indeed a product of that situation, not as one who is simply its effect, but as it "lives" its situation. To "live" a situation is not to transcend it by being external to it, but to suffer it or endure it, to repeat it in some fashion or work to modify it. The grounds for the latter are in the felt contradictions of the situation formative of the subject. Were there no felt contradictions, for Sartre there would be no critical project. But contradictions, to be felt or lived, imply the psychically split subject.

We have adverted to Butler's rejection of phenomenology, that she thinks it unsurpassably dualistic. To say that the subject is "situated" is not enough. The subject, for Butler, "is an accomplishment regulated and produced in advance" (FC 47). And yet the subject is not merely, for her, a passive effect, but rather "the permanent possibility of a certain resignifying process" (FC 47). Instead of appealing, as does Sartre, to the nature of lived experience to ground the "irreducibility" of the subject to the fixity of identity, Butler turns to discourse itself, "the illimitable process of signification itself" (GT 143). Language neither creates nor coincides with existence. It is in the distance/difference of language from existence that a play between them becomes possible:

> The linguistic categories that are understood to "denote" the materiality of the body are themselves troubled by a referent that is never fully or permanently resolved or contained by any given signified. Indeed, that referent persists only as a kind of absence or loss, that which language does not capture, but, instead, that which impels language repeatedly to attempt that capture, that circumscription— and to fail. This loss takes its place in language as an insistent call or demand that, while *in* language, is never fully *of* language. (BTM 67)

Both the complex relationship that obtains between significations ("the ideality of differentiating relations") and the indirectness of reference guarantee the failure of discursive determination of identity. The "excess" of the discursive is the irreducibility of language's other. Social interpellations attempt to produce an identity between word and reality which is impossible. As a result, the impossible identity can figure only as a norm or ideal to be constrained through law, prohibition, threat, taboo, fear of punishment, and so forth, constraints which can work only through citation. The subject is thus a "site" of productive power, a forming or making of a certain body, as well as of the failure of that production to realize its end thoroughly. The result is a site of permanent instability and potential contestation or creative recitation.

Sartre's and Butler's accounts of identity are not the same. They are written in different registers, phenomenological and post-structuralist. Yet significant parallel features lead me to look at both as existentialist accounts that offer a version of the subject as an ongoing process both immersed in social conditions and ultimately called to account for them by realizing its capacity for self-invention. In making this assessment I heavily rely on Sartre's later work, which he himself characterized by a statement with which I believe Butler would concur: "This is the limit I would today accord to freedom: the small movement which makes of a totally conditioned social being someone who does not render back completely what his conditioning has given him" (IT 35). Both Sartre's and Butler's critiques of identity—driven, respectively, by phenomenological and poststructuralist versions of difference—are political acts offering hope to victims of oppressive social structures. In this regard, I think that Butler's judgment that phenomenological versions of the subject are "politically insidious" is misplaced. In Sartre's case, his work remains a powerful indictment of oppressive regimes of various sorts. While Butler's work on identity is already something of a "classic," her political (and ethical?) philosophy is still developing. It remains to be seen whether the depiction of the subject as an agential "site" of reconfiguration is enough to support the more recent venture, or whether she will need to flesh out a richer sense of self, one such as is present in the personal narrative of the prefaces to *Gender Trouble* and *Bodies That Matter* wherein the site takes on a name, personal history, and rebellious expression that gives these wonderful books experiential context. Lacking that context, the tightly argued diagnostic analysis of the book would, for me, lose its political, and ethical, force. The narrative prefaces do not simply describe, but warn the reader of "trouble," a trouble first detected in lived experience, in suffering and conflict, and then circulated in analysis for response. The analysis bears on the lived impact of social structures, and the entire "message" of the books constitutes a call for change. As we shall soon see, this is, for Sartre, the function of literature—to carry lives, broken from sheer metaphysical identity, into the circulation of words to others for their response. In any case, Butler's work is, for me, an exciting and interesting project, prolonging deep existential resonances into the poststructuralist philosophical scene.

## WORKS OF SARTRE CITED

BN      *Being and Nothingness*. Trans. Hazel Barnes. New York: Philosophical Library, 1956 (*L'Être et le néant*. Paris: Gallimard, 1943).

CDR    *Critique of Dialectical Reason.* Vol. 1. Trans. Alan Sheridan-Smith. London: Humanities Press, 1976 (*Critique de la raison dialectique.* Vol. 1. Paris: Gallimard, 1960).

F    *The Flies.* In *No Exit and Three Other Plays.* Trans. Stuart Gilbert. New York: Vintage International, 1989 (*Les Mouches.* Paris: Gallimard, 1943).

FI    *The Family Idiot.* Vols. 1–2. Trans. Carol Cosman. Chicago: University of Chicago Press, 1981, 1987 (*L'Idiot de la famille.* Vol. 1. Paris: Gallimard, 1971).

IT    *"The Itinerary of a Thought."* In *Jean-Paul Sartre: Between Existentialism and Marxism,* trans. John Mathews, 33–64. New York: Morrow, 1974.

PFI    *"A Plea for Intellectuals."* In *Jean-Paul Sartre: Between Existentialism and Marxism,* trans. John Mathews, 228–85. New York: Morrow, 1974.

SG    *Saint Genet: Actor and Martyr.* Trans. Bernard Frechtman. New York: Mentor, 1963 (*Saint Genet: Comédien et martyre.* Paris: Gallimard, 1952).

SM    *Search for a Method.* Trans. Hazel Barnes. New York: Vintage, 1968 (*Questions de méthode.* Paris: Gallimard, 1967).

TE    *The Transcendence of the Ego.* Trans. Forrest Williams and Robert Kirkpatrick. New York: Noonday Press, 1957 (*La Transcendance de l'Égo: Esquisse d'une théorie phénoménologique.* Paris: Vrin, 1965).

## Works of Butler Cited

BTM    *Bodies That Matter.* New York: Routledge, 1993.

FC    "Contingent Foundations." In *Feminist Contentions,* by Seyla Benhabib, Judith Butler, Drucilla Cornell, and Nancy Fraser, 35–57. New York: Routledge, 1995.

GT    *Gender Trouble.* New York: Routledge, 1990.

PI    "Variations on Sex and Gender: Beauvoir, Wittig, and Foucault." *Praxis International* 5 (January 1986): 505–16.

SD    *Subjects of Desire: Hegelian Reflections in Twentieth-Century France.* New York: Columbia University Press, 1987.

SSR    "Subjection, Resistance, Resignification: Between Freud and Foucault." In *The Identity in Question,* ed. John Rajch-man, 229–49. New York: Routledge, 1995.

## NOTE

I wish to express my gratitude to Alan Schrift, who allowed me to study his paper "Performance Check: A Brief Genealogy and Some Questions for Judith Butler," presented at the annual meeting of the Society for Phenomenology and Existential Philosophy at its 1996 meeting at Georgetown University.

# 4

# Sartre on Language and Politics (with Reference to Particularity)

FROM THE TIME Jean-Paul Sartre was six years old, when he began to read and discovered his grandfather's library, until his death, words were the element in which he existed. His slim volume of autobiography, *The Words* (1963), featured only two divisions: reading and writing. If we add to the time covered by the autobiography his subsequent blindness, another section, listening to words, would complete the story. He wrote on almost every art, proposing a general ontology of art objects in *The Psychology of Imagination* (1940), producing essays on the mobiles of Caldor, Giacometti's statues, the paintings of Tintoretto, the poems of Baudelaire and Mallarmé, and even a piece on music. But writers and writing were his special, almost obsessive interest: Faulkner, Dos Passos, Gide, Genet, Kafka, Sarraute . . . Yet when he formed his technical philosophy, language itself was, as a theme, almost neglected. In *Being and Nothingness* (1943), language is relegated to a few pages, treated as a side issue in discussions of the body, techniques, and inauthenticity. His views on language and writing took shape within the broader context of his philosophy of consciousness, with its heavy stress upon psychological life.

Sartre's early ontology is dominated by the power of individual consciousness to give meaning to a world through its unconditioned choices. Language is understood to be a tool for the free meaning-giving consciousness. The basis of language usage is, for Sartre, the sentence, for it is here that consciousness imbues language with meaning: "Since the verbal unity is the meaningful sentence, the latter is a constructive act which is conceived only by a transcendence which surpasses and nihilates the given toward an end" (BN 515). Phonemes, morphemes, syntax, and lexical meanings are "givens," facticity which the free self surpasses in creating its own personal meanings. While insisting that free subjectivity is a factical being in the world ("The for-itself is free but *in condition*"), Sartre holds at the same time that "choice is always unconditioned," that "the given in no way enters into the constitution of freedom" (BN 519, 479, 487). *Being and Nothingness* valiantly tries to hold together the discourses of situatedness and transcendence in an attempt to avoid the impasses of idealism and realism, but privileged stress is on transcendence, often to the point of courting idealism. "Each for-itself, in fact, is a for-itself only by choosing itself beyond nationality and race just as it speaks beyond syntax and morphemes. This 'beyond' is enough to assure its total independence in relation to the structures which it surpasses" (BN 520). The depiction of surpassing the given (nationality, race, language) in terms of "total independence" and the refusal to admit the conditioning of subjectivity by the given breaks the tension between situation and transcendence in favor of a dualism. In discussing how a free consciousness "interiorizes" a technique for its purposes, Sartre emphasizes how the technique is integrated into the subjective project: "The For-itself surpasses the technique toward its own end" (BN 523). He then proceeds to claim that in the process the technique "loses its character as a technique and is integrated purely and simply in the free surpassing of the given toward it ends" (BN 523). This psychologism with regard to the technique implies that the technique loses its structure, and the effect of that structure on the subjectivity that employs it, simply because subjectivity is unaware of that structure. Sartre's eagerness to protect the autonomy of the self leads him in this way to weaken the insistence which runs throughout *Being and Nothingness* on the thorough situatedness of subjectivity. Sartre's treatment, or nontreatment, of language in his ontology speaks to the failure of *Being and Nothingness* to deal seriously with institutions and, in general, the role played by shared discursive and praxical background in identity formation. Subsequent to *Being and Nothingness* he would attempt to redress this weakness.

In the midst of his brief discussion of language as a technique in *Being and Nothingness,* Sartre pauses to mention a view of language of which he has recently become aware: "It has been maintained recently that there is a sort of living order of words, of the

dynamic laws of speech, an impersonal life of the logos—in short
that speech is a Nature and that to some extent man must obey it
in order to make use of it as he does with Nature" (BN 516). In
a footnote he cites as representing this view Brice Parain's *Essai
sur le logos platonicien*. Not long after the publication of *Being and
Nothingness,* Sartre wrote a lengthy essay, "Departure and Return," on Parain's book *Recherche sur la nature et la fonction du lan-
gage*. Sartre was clearly bothered by Parain's views, since they had
the effect of decentering the very powers of the self that Sartre
was intent on inflating. In his essay, Sartre goes into a more de-
tailed account of the relation of the conscious subject to language
than he had presented in *Being and Nothingness,* an account heavily
influenced by Husserl's transcendentalism. He asks how a word is
recognized to be the same word, how it has an objective identity,
so that one can use it again and again. How can, say, the word
"pellet" be endowed with an identity so that I recognize it as the
same word that struck me yesterday and that strikes me today? To
use or understand such a word, Sartre argues, "I would have to
recognize it, that is, to extract it from the flux of phenomena and
stabilize it. I would still have to refer it to its appearances of yesterday and the day before and establish between these different
meanings a synthetic place of identification" (LPE 170). Knowledge and communication are possible because of "syntheses of
identification" effected by the subject: "It is I who, either in listening or speaking, establish the word" (LPE 171). The amplifi-
cation of Sartre's views on language in "Departure and Return"
serve to point out how important it was to him to establish the
subject's control over meaning. Perhaps one can appreciate why
when language is considered within the psychoanalytic context of
*Being and Nothingness*.

The role of existential psychoanalysis in *Being and Nothingness*
is pivotal in assessing the book's identity, which has often escaped
commentators. While the ontological distinctions between being-
for-itself, being-in-itself, and being-for-others are central, it is important to note their place within the dramatic background of bad
faith and authenticity. Difference, in the form of *néant,* is at the
heart of the drama, for *néant* breaks up the identity of being. *Néant*
is formative of the self (being-for-itself), which is defined as "a
being which effects in itself a break in being." The break in iden-

tity constitutive of the self is the self-awareness that produces the self as at a distance from itself and from what is other than itself. Considered from one angle, the self as nonsubstantial is a failure to be one with itself and its environment. From another angle, that very failure is freedom, since, for Sartre, such a self is not locked into any particular identity. Lacking deep metaphysical identity, the self can only perform or act out identities. The dramatic backdrop to the ontology concerns bad faith. As a lack or loss of identity, the self is haunted by the dream of achieving identity, which would have the effect, Sartre says, of overcoming contingency, of being a self-foundation. But this is, by the terms of Sartre's ontological definitions, impossible. Faced with the desire for the impossible, the self turns to the ruse of belief, a strategy whereby the self attempts to convince itself of being its (lacking) identity. Much of *Being and Nothingness* is given to tracking down various types of bad faith, which can give the reader the impression that all that life amounts to is a vain attempt to reach the impossible. However, Sartre provides many hints that such is not the case, and this is why psychoanalysis is so important to the story he is telling in *Being and Nothingness*. Psychoanalysis is a hermeneutic of action and desire which, as developed by Sartre, permits one to recognize oneself as failed desire and to consciously choose oneself as freedom, as lack, as a contingent perspective among other contingent perspectives. Existential psychoanalysis is the prelude to conversion from bad faith to authenticity. *Being and Nothingness* is a therapeutic proposal which, while detailing forms of bad faith and offering a way out of bad faith (he uses the term "salvation"), provides no details regarding the authentic life. This is why "What Is Literature?" (1947) is so important, marking as it does Sartre's turn toward fleshing out authenticity in terms of ethics and politics, and doing so by highlighting language.

While Sartre's sketchy pronouncements on language in *Being and Nothingness* formed the background of his discussion of literature, he was constrained to nuance them in sorting out literature from the other arts—in particular, to distinguish poetry and prose from one another. In ordinary communication, in their designative function, words are, we are told by Sartre, "transparent," melting, as it were, into their designative function (exemplifying his view that in usage a technique "loses its character as a technique"). Prose engages language precisely in this designative or "utilitarian" function. The prose writer "is a *speaker:* he designates, demonstrates, orders, refuses, interpolates, begs, insults, persuades, insinuates" (WIL 34). This radically separates, in Sartre's estimation, the prose writer from the poet. In poetry words are not simply designators, but are "things" that draw attention to themselves, to their look and sound and feel. Poets intercept the transparency of words, for they use words as painters use colors and composers sounds. Poetry uses words as objects to induce images, whereas prose writers use words as designators, revealers of the world.

In revealing the lived world, the prose writer raises it to a thematic level where it is presented to others for their response. Literature, as communicative, is a dialectic between writer and reader wherein each recognizes the freedom of the other, affording a glimpse into a positive reciprocity in human relationships which was lacking in *Being and Nothingness.* The expressive and communicative nature of literature implies an ideal community, a collaborative use of freedoms, "the conjoint effort of author and reader," wherein "the writer appeals to the reader's freedom to collaborate in the production of his work" (WIL 51, 54).) In addressing his or her work to readers, the writer assumes their freedom, their powers to reproduce the aesthetic object, while readers, in picking up the author's work, implicitly recognize the author's creative powers. Literature is thus a "co-creation," a shared responsibility for bringing the aesthetic object into being.

The ideal community implicated in the collaborative process in literature is referred to as Kant's "City of Ends":

> Let us bear in mind that the man who reads strips himself in some way of his empirical personality and escapes from his resentments, his fears, and his lusts in order to put himself at the peak of his freedom. This freedom takes the literary work and, through it, mankind, for absolute ends. It sets itself up as an unconditioned exigence in relationship to itself, to the author, and to its possible readers. It can therefore be identified with Kantian *good will* which, in every circumstance, treats man as an end and not as a means. Thus, by his very exigence, the reader attains that chorus of good wills which Kant has called the City of Ends, which thousands of

readers all over the world who do not know each other are, at every moment, helping to maintain. (WIL 218–19)

Because the community here depicted is based on mutual recognition, adopting postures of address and response as the very condition of the possibility of literature, then, Sartre concludes, "it would be inconceivable that this unleashing of generosity provoked by the writer could be used to authorize an injustice, and the reader could enjoy his freedom while reading a book which approves or accepts or simply abstains from condemning the subjection of man by man" (WIL 67). The ideal communicative fraternity exemplified in literature serves as the Sartrean ideal of authenticity in morality and politics. The latter concerns the processes of realizing this community in concrete circumstances, the attempt to historicize "abstract good wills" into "material and timely demands."

Sartre distinguishes between an actual and a virtual audience for a literary work. The virtual audience is composed of all who can possibly read and respond to the work, while the actual audience consists of those who, under specific historical conditions, know how to read, have access to books, and so forth. Much of "What Is Literature?" is devoted to a discussion of various historical periods which shows the impact of class structure on the actual life of literature, how only certain people were actually able to participate in the process, and how, in Sartre's eyes, this constitutes a distortion of ideal literary communication. Using examples taken from the practices of writing in the twelfth, seventeenth, eighteenth, and nineteenth centuries, he attempts to display the contradiction between the ideal and universal reach of literature (its "essence") and its particular historical realizations and alienation. The "clerk" of the twelfth century was co-opted by the institution of the Church for its purposes. Seventeenth-century writers wrote for the gentry, who required pleasing images of themselves. The newly emerging bourgeois writers of the eighteenth century glowingly wrote of "universal man," while identifying it with a particular class. In the next century the bourgeois writer became aware of this contradiction, but renounced exploring it in favor of the escapist illusion of "art for art's sake." He concludes by pointing out the discrepancy between the essence of literature and the practice of literature:

The examples we have chosen have served only to *situate* the freedom of the writer in different ages, to illuminate by the limits of
the demands made upon him the limits of his appeal, to show by
the idea of his role which the public fashions for itself the necessary
boundaries of the idea he invents of literature. And if it is true that
the essence of the literary work is freedom totally disclosing and
willing itself as an appeal to the freedom of men, it is also true that
the different forms of oppression, by hiding from men the fact that
they were free, have screened all or part of that essence from au-
thors. (WIL 133)

For Sartre, there is only one way to bring actual societal life
into conformity with the demands of the ideal community of
literature: "In essence, *actual* literature can only realize its full *essence* in a classless society" (WIL 189). There is, in his reasoning,
an inherent telos in communicative understanding which passes
through the Kantian imperative to treat others as unconditioned
ends to the Marxist imperative to change society by eliminating
classes. His account of the ideal "essence" of literature serves as
the critical lever, in "What Is Literature?" for translating the
vague forecasts of authenticity in *Being and Nothingness* into more
concrete form. But in the process, the analysis in "What Is Literature?" comes to reflect in its own way the tension we have already noted in *Being and Nothingness* between ontological and
situational understandings of freedom. In "What Is Literature?"
the tension is between the ideal essence of literature and situational (social and historical) facticity. The former, idealizing an
undistorted communicative situation, leads Sartre to utopian rhet-
oric about the "reign of freedom." There is an idealist streak in
Sartre which, although tamed to some extent over the years by
persistent thinking against himself, proves at times irrepressible.
Even in his later years, when he knew better, he would lapse into
talk about the possibility (and desirability) of "transparency" in
human relationships: "I think transparency should always be substituted for secrecy. . . . A man's existence must be entirely visible
to his neighbor, whose own existence must be entirely visible in
turn, before true social harmony can be established" (L/S 11).
"What Is Literature?" is a work given to utopianism in its call for
"total freedom," which is "the freedom of changing everything;
which means besides suppression of classes, abolition of all dicta-

torship, constant renewal of frameworks, and the continuous overthrowing of order once it tends to congeal" (WIL 139). Commitment to total freedom justified extensive violence in Sartre's eyes because any lack of transparency was, from his point of view, the result of bad will. This directly issues from his view of language as a transparency, of how language is a tool constituted and controlled by each consciousness, of how meaning is an affair of consciousness and its intentions.

Shortly after the publication of "What Is Literature?" Sartre modified his position that poetry was apolitical. He wrote "Black Orpheus" as the preface to Leopold Sedar Senghor's *Anthologie de la nouvelle poésie nègre et malgache de langue française,* published in 1948 (and reprinted in *Situations III* in 1949). Here Sartre proclaims that "black poetry in the French language is, in our time, the only great revolutionary poetry" (BO 295). The French colonizer has set itself up in the minds of the colonized through teaching them the French language. "And since words are ideas, when the Negro declares in French that he rejects French culture, he accepts with one hand what he rejects with the other" (BO 301). The French language, Sartre points out, reflects a historical collectivity. It has been forged over time to respond to specific, contingent needs and circumstances, and is "unsuitable" to furnish the Negro "with the means of speaking about himself, his own anxieties, his own hopes" (BO 301). For the Negro to speak prose, a straightforward use of words, would be to fail to speak the Negro's experience. Poetry allows for a speaking of experience that simultaneously performs an "autodestruction of language": "The black herald is going to *deFrenchify* [words]; he will crush them, break their usual associations, he will violently couple them" (BO 303). The poet will use words to "evoke" and "suggest" and "incant" a "silence" beyond the words, the silence of the experience of colonized negritude. This revelatory silence functions as did prose in "What Is Literature?"—as a presentation of the world for purposes of evaluation and change.

In "Black Orpheus," Sartre displays a sensitivity toward language's being, its thickness, its historical contingency, the specificity of its meanings as opposed to its "transparency." At the same time, he appears to suggest that this deference to the particular and contingent was a moment of dialectical transiency. The black herald's stubborn protestation of his or her particular experience is only a temporal phase, a dialectical moment, to be transcended in a future universal synthesis: "It is when negritude renounces itself that it finds itself; it is when it accepts losing that it has won: the colored man—and he alone—can be asked to renounce the pride of his color. He is the one who is walking on this ridge between past particularism—which he has just climbed—and future universalism, which will be the twilight of his negritude; he is the one who looks to the end of particularism in order to find the dawn of the universal" (BO 328–29). Sartre views the black poets' works to be encompassed by the tension between the particular and the universal which haunts "What Is Literature?" As works of art, these revolutionary poems are "a call to the spectator's liberty and absolute generosity" (BO 330) and thus implicate the ideal City of Ends and a universal freedom. Their works, with all their specificity, are "grafted," Sartre tells us, "onto another branch of the universal Revolution" (BO 313).

The closest Sartre came to rewriting "What Is Literature?" is "A Plea for Intellectuals," an address he presented on a trip to Japan in 1965, which can be read as a response to criticism of "What Is Literature?" by Merleau-Ponty (and Roland Barthes in his *Writing Degree Zero* as well). In 1948 Merleau-Ponty wrote an unpublished commentary on "What Is Literature?" in which he concluded: "I must do a sort of 'What Is Literature?' with a longer section on the sign and prose."[1] Many of the ideas sketched out in these unpublished notes find their way into *The Prose of the World*, culminating in the essay first drafted for that work and later published in slightly revised form in *Signs* as "Indirect Language and the Voices of Silence," dedicated to Sartre. At the beginning of the essay, Merleau-Ponty challenges Sartre's view of language as a tool: "Language is much more like a sort of being than a means."[2] This claim against Sartre of the thickness as opposed to the transparency of language has the effect, for Merleau-Ponty, of putting literature and the other arts on a similar footing. Thus, the essay both is and is not about painting as expression and communication. There are "echoes" in painting of all forms of expression, and even "political thought itself is of this order,"[3] the order of the life of expression and communication. He agrees with Sartre that an ethics of mutual respect and recognition is implied in communication. "At the moment of expression," Merleau-Ponty tells us, "the other to whom I address myself and I who express myself are incontestably linked together."[4] The "call" or "appeal" implied in expression is a recognition of the other, and the other's response is recognition of myself. Merleau-Ponty emphatically disagrees with Sartre's conception of the transparency of language, with its presumption of the intentional control of meaning by the expressing subject. For Merleau-Ponty this smacks of the phenomenological notion of the constitution of meaning, a view that, for him, represses the role of institutions in the formation of meaning. Meaning, according to Merleau-Ponty, is embedded in institutions, traditions, enduring forms of life in which subjects are thoroughly implicated. When subjects express and communicate with one another it is in terms of this enduring meaning, which both forms their expression and is carried forward and across diverse forms of enduring meaning by them. Throughout his essay, Merleau-Ponty emphasizes how, in his understanding, meaning in communication is inevitably pluralistic, ambiguous, contingent, unfinished, undermining any tendency toward a utopian notion of ideal agreement based on univocal understanding of meaning and its univocal application.

At first contact, "A Plea for Intellectuals" appears continuous with "What Is Literature?" when we meet the "technician," who is an updated version of the medieval clerk, that is, one who has the special skills or knowledges necessary for the conducting of institutional business. Technicians are institutional functionaries of a thoroughly secularized world, "a new stratum of 'experts' [who] arose from within the ranks of the bourgeoisie; they constituted neither a class nor an elite, but were wholly integrated in the vast enterprise that was mercantile capitalism, and provided it with the means to self-production and expansion" (PFI 233). These specialists of knowledge were the technical functionaries, constantly evolving in degree of expertise as necessary for a developing technology (scientists, engineers, accountants, doctors, lawyers, ideological apologists), for bourgeois capitalism. Such experts are produced by and co-opted for institutional purposes, which are rationalized as humanitarian, but consist of profit and utility alone. Sartre argues that the social being of these technicians involves a contradiction, which is the potential basis for be-

coming an "intellectual," for whom the contradiction becomes
alienation and the basis of developing resistance to the status quo:

> [Technicians of knowledge] function as researchers equipped with
> specific knowledges and methods. They are universalist because
> they seek universal forms of knowledge and practice. But if they
> apply their methods to an examination of the ruling class and its
> ideology—which is *their own*—they cannot hide from themselves
> the fact that both are surreptitiously particularist. At that moment
> they discover alienation: they become aware that they are the in-
> struments of ends which remain foreign to them and which they
> are forbidden to question. (PFI 241)

Sartre cites as an example technicians of health, whose knowledge
is universalist (involving the principles of health as such, experts
of the digestive tract, circulatory system, etc.), yet whose practice
is particularist in the delivery of health, treating the digestive tracts
and circulatory systems of a certain segment of society. The technician of knowledge becomes an intellectual, for Sartre, with the
recognition of contradiction, by appreciating it as alienation, and
with the resolve to universalize practice. The contradiction in the
social being of the intellectual raises problems for Sartre's treasured "transparency" of consciousness, for as a product of society,
the technician is conditioned in thought, suffering from "class
prejudices inculcated in him since childhood, even while it believed itself to be free of them and to have attained the universal"
(PFI 249). The intellectual must therefore work to modify him-
or herself while working to change social conditions. Because of
this social facticity, the intellectual must try to "adopt the point
of view of the most underprivileged members. . . . The only
way the intellectual can really distance himself from the official
ideology decreed from above is by placing himself alongside those
whose very existence contradicts it" (PFI 255). The intellectual
must intervene "at the level of events," unmasking ideology, producing events to counteract specific injustices, using one's knowledge "concretely" to serve the oppressed. But the intellectual
must preserve a critical function to the point of revealing and
opposing misuse of power even among the oppressed. The intellectual will live "*in tension*," between the privileged who consider
him or her a traitor and the oppressed who suspect him or her of
being an outsider, tainted by privilege.

The discussion of the technician/intellectual reflects the tension between the universal and the particular in "What Is Literature?" In that work, it was a case of the universalist ideal of reciprocal recognition of freedoms between writer and reader versus the particularist instantiation of writing and reading in historical circumstances. The political consequence called for is a democratic socialist society, a historical realization of the abstract City of Ends, wherein the virtual, universalist recognition of freedoms is actualized in a society of real equality. "A Plea for Intellectuals," while continuing the discourse of universal and particular, does so in a much more concrete manner than "What Is Literature?"—one which stresses the weight of the particular. It is evident that Sartre is abandoning the abstract subjectivity of his early ontology for a concrete subjectivity that claims a history and genealogy. Heavily influenced by the *cogito* tradition in his early work, Sartre founded critique in the power of consciousness to detach itself from its situation, to question even its own identity and to remake itself and its environment in the light of its subjective possibilities. In "A Plea for Intellectuals," he is reconceiving critique as he reconceives subjectivity. The technician is a product of society, and the possibility of critique lies in the contradiction immanent in the social being of the technician. The recognition of this social facticity makes Sartre a bit wary, however, with regard to discourse about realizing the universal: "All those who adopt a universalist perspective *here and now* are *reassuring* to the established order. . . . The human universal is yet to come" (PFI 253). Not even the "universal" proletariat of Marx represent the universal as the intellectual forms its other, as we have observed. With regard to intellectuals themselves, "perpetual contradictions and dissensions are the lot of the social group we call intellectuals" (PFI 263). Despite this recognition of how deep differences in social facticity run, Sartre retains his hope for realizing a "social universality . . . where all men will be *truly* free, equal and fraternal" (PFI 254), without spelling out any future role of differences in this universality.

In the final section of "A Plea for Intellectuals," Sartre returns to the major themes of "What Is Literature?"—writing and the writer—this time (yielding to Merleau-Ponty's critique) beginning with the citation of the "materiality" and "density" of words: "One might say that the *word* tends both to point vaguely in the direction of the signified and to impose itself as a *presence,* drawing the reader's attention to its own density. This is why it has been possible for people to say that to name something means both to *present* the signified and to kill or bury it in the mass of the word" (PFI 270). Words and language have an irreducible facticity, structural and historical, which both makes communication possible and troubles its "ideal." Language, Sartre admits, is "something *other* than the writer and *other* than men" (PFI 270). While not at all denying that language refers, Sartre now admits that reference is never direct and unambiguous. All writing suffers the "narcissism" he formerly located in poetry as opposed to prose. Following Merleau-Ponty, Sartre concedes that all literary communication is indirect and allusive:

> The writer can testify only to his own being-in-the-world, by pro-
> ducing an ambiguous object which suggests it allusively. Thus the
> real relationship between reader and writer remains non-knowl-
> edge: when reading a writer's work, the reader is referred back
> indirectly to his reality as a singular universal. He realizes himself—
> both because he enters into the book and does not completely enter
> into it—as another part of the same whole, as another point of view
> of the world on itself. (PFI 277)

Communication in writing is a matter of charging the "significa-tions" of language with "meanings," which are existential and contextual. The point of writing is still to "reveal" the world, to offer it for evaluation, but now the process of revelation appears from the earlier perspective of "What Is Literature?" to be com-promised by language itself as a system of public meanings which are as it were, in themselves, plurivocal, having a weight and his-tory. The writer must present his or her lived situation in language and, Sartre holds, "beyond language." The existential meaning conveyed by writing appears only obliquely: "The writer chooses to use ordinary language not *in spite of* this material weight but *because of it.* His art lies in his ability to attract the reader's attention to the materiality of any given word, even while conveying as exactly as possible a meaning through it, so that the object signi-fied is at once beyond the word and yet incarnated in its material-ity" (PFI 279). The writer's attempt to evoke a concrete situation in the reader is, in turn, dependent upon the reader's ability to cooperate, to lend his or her own experience ("the reader is referred back indirectly to his own reality as a singular universal"), which is never perfectly coincidental with that of the writer, producing an inevitable interpretation instead of a repetition of meaning ("because he enters into the book and does not completely enter into it"), what Merleau-Ponty called an inevitable "deformation of meaning."

The world is, first of all, *lived,* and lived from a singular perspective, while at the same time being shaped by universal structures. Sartre refuses to dissolve individuals into structures, and he is using writing as a model to display his conception of the singular universal, a non-reductive model of understanding the structure/ individual relationship, for writing, as literature, involves language as structure and individual experience. To the extent that structures operate and persist through language, they are subject to interpretation and modification. Sartre rejects a deterministic account of structure and individual in favor of a hermeneutic account. Human existence as a "singular universal" finds itself to be both socially produced and structured on the one hand and lived individually and contingently in a process of internalization and externalization on the other. This does not mean that structures are external to individuals and lived experience, but that structures function only as lived, as inevitably interpreted by those who live them in the contingent and complex circumstances of concrete life.

While "A Plea for Intellectuals" sustains the discourse of the mutual recognition of freedoms implied in the function of literature, it bows to ambiguity, particularity, and the inevitable plurality of interpretation in such communication. Clear and undistorted communication in literature, which would result in univocal understanding, is an unreal expectation, undercutting the utopianism of "What Is Literature?" Because words as such are only "quasi-meanings" (universal) until applied from and to lived experience (particular), particularity is irreducible in concrete understanding: "The quasi-meanings suggested by a work have significance (*sens*) as objective structures of the social, only if they appear to be concrete because lived from a particular anchorage. An objective universal will never be attained by a work

of literature: but it remains the horizon of an effort of universalization" (PFI 283). Since literature remains the model Sartre employs for thinking about politics, this admission is enormously
telling. He is not simply warning us to be on guard against being
bewitched by false universals. Rather, he is rejecting the notion
of a universal that would surpass all particularity. The "task of the
writer," he tells us, "is to remain on the level of lived experience
while suggesting *universalization* as the affirmation of life on its
*horizon*" (PFI 284). But the universal will always be on the "horizon," never realized. It remains a perpetual "task." Universality
is "ongoing universalization," for Sartre continues to hold that
in its "essence" literature tends toward the universal, while now
recognizing the inevitable and unsurpassable role of facticity and
contingency in the concrete functioning of literature.

In "Black Orpheus," Sartre spoke of the black poet as "one
who looks to the end of particularism in order to find the dawn
of the universal" (BO 329). This is reflective of an understanding
of dialectic in which the particular is surpassed into the universal:
"It is the dialectical law of successive transformations which lead
the Negro to coincidence with himself in negritude," under the
proviso that "negritude is *for* destroying itself; it is a 'crossing to'
and not an 'arrival at,' a means and not an end" (BO 327). Sartre
contributed another preface to a political book in 1971, when he
wrote "The Burgos Trial" for Gisele Halimi's *Procès de Burgos*.
Here one finds a different, non-reductive relationship of universal
and particular, reflective of the changes evident in "A Plea for
Intellectuals." The Burgos trial concerns the issue of Basque sepa-
ratism, which Sartre uses to attack the "abstract universalism" of
Left and Right. "The Spanish exploit the Basques *because they are
Basques*. Without ever admitting it officially, they are convinced
that the Basques are *other*, both ethnically and culturally" (BT
147). "In this sense," he continues, "Basque culture today must
be first of all a counterculture. It is created by destroying Spanish
culture, by rejecting the universalist humanism of the central
powers, by making a constant and mighty effort to reclaim Basque
reality" (BT 150). "Universal humanism" is, for Sartre, based
upon a "type of abstract man" which is oppressively utilized to
reduce what is different under the guise of "unity": "Behind the
unity which is such a source of pride to the great powers is op-

pression of ethnic groups and the hidden or open use of repression" (BT 137). Sartre spends a good bit of time tracing out the history of the repression of the Basques and their strategies and tactics for reclaiming their reality. He sympathizes with their plight and sees in them "a glimpse of *another* kind of socialism," one which reflects his understanding of the "singular universal." The political is inseparable from the cultural, which represents the particular: "What the ETA [Independence Party] reveals to us is the need of *all* men, even centralists, to affirm their particularities against abstract universality. To listen to the voices of the Basques, the Bretons, the Occitanians, and to struggle beside them so that they may affirm their concrete singularity, is to fight for ourselves as well" (BT 161). Here one finds no surpassing of the particular into the universal, but rather an attempt to reconceive the goals of an ideal City of Ends (freedom, reciprocity) in a way that recognizes the irreducible facticity and particularity of the concrete.

William McBride, in his admirable study *Sartre's Political Theory,* made the following observation about Sartre's later political views: "Whereas readers of the *Critique* had cause to wonder just how seriously Sartre might be regarding the possibility of a definitive, Apocalyptic movement that would bring the progressive development of history's totalization into clear focus once and for all, Sartre's remarks of this late period of his life make perfectly evident that he regards such a notion as a fairy tale."[5] McBride goes on to characterize what he sees as the reasons for this: "Polyvalence of meanings, extreme tentativeness except with respect to the ultimate, simultaneously libertarian and communitarian revolutionary goals: the Sartre of the last active years is in many respects *un homme postmoderne.*"[6] In forming this estimation, McBride gives serious weight to the controversial conversations Sartre had with Benny Levy, published shortly before Sartre's death, in which he stressed the significance of institutions, traditions, fraternity, the interpenetration of ethics, culture, and politics. What Sartre is expressing in these interviews is the result of his philosophical development over the years, as exemplified in the changes we have observed from "What Is Literature?" to "A Plea for Intellectuals." Language and literary communication formed the model for his conception of ethical and political community, and his understanding of the latter changed with the evolution of his views on the former. His thinking on language evolved from considering it as "transparency" to "ambiguity," from subjective control and creation to strategic dialectic, from surpassing the particular to recognizing its irreducibility.

All social change occurs within a particular context with a contingency of its own which must be taken into account. "In fact," Sartre has said, "when human society would have overcome its divisions and achieved a socialism of abundance, it would still be the case, at the heart of its internal necessity, that it has been constituted on the basis of original contingency, not by eliminating it but by integrating it into its own order."[7] The integration is not a dissolution of contingency, for the lesson of "The Burgos Trial" was "the profound transformation which decentralization can help bring about in the thinking of centralized socialism" (BT 139). Specificity and locality are, for Sartre, inevitably part of all thought and action. There is, McBride reminds us, no one formula, no one solution, even if there is a common goal—a democratic society. It is not a question of reducing either the particular or the universal, but of thinking them together.

## WORKS OF SARTRE CITED

BN    *Being and Nothingness*. Trans. Hazel Barnes. New York: Philosophical Library, 1956 (*L'Être et le néant*. Paris: Gallimard, 1943).

BO    "Black Orpheus." Trans. John MacCombie. In *What Is Literature? and Other Essays*, 291–330. Cambridge: Harvard University Press, 1988 ("Orphée noir." In *Situations*. Vol. 3. Paris: Gallimard, 1949).

BT    "The Burgos Trial." In *Life/Situations: Essays Written and Spoken*, trans. Paul Auster and Lydia Davis, 135–61. New York: Pantheon Books, 1977 (*Situations*. Vol. 10. Paris: Gallimard, 1977).

LPE   "Departure and Return." In *Literary and Philosophical Essays*, trans. Annette Michelson, 133–79. New York: Collier, 1962.

L/S   "Self-Portrait at Seventy." In *Life/Situations: Essays Writ-*

*ten and Spoken,* trans. Paul Auster and Lydia Davis, 3–92. New York: Pantheon, 1977.

PFI  "A Plea for Intellectuals." In *Jean-Paul Sartre,* trans. John Mathews, 228–85. New York: Morrow, 1974.

WIL  "What Is Literature?" Trans. Bernard Frechtman. In *What Is Literature? and Other Essays,* 25–238. Cambridge: Harvard University Press, 1988 ("Qu'est-ce que la littérature?" In *Situations.* Vol. 2. Paris: Gallimard, 1948).

## NOTES

1. Maurice Merleau-Ponty, *The Prose of the World,* ed. Claude Lefort, trans. John O'Neill (Evanston, Ill.: Northwestern University Press, 1973), xvi. See Lefort's preface for his comments with reference to Merleau-Ponty's unpublished commentary on "What Is Literature?"

2. Maurice Merleau-Ponty, "Indirect Language and the Voices of Silence," *Signs,* trans. Richard McCleary (Evanston, Ill.: Northwestern University Press, 1964), 43.

3. Ibid., 83.

4. Ibid., 73.

5. William McBride, *Sartre's Political Theory* (Bloomington: Indiana University Press, 1991), 191.

6. Ibid., 192.

7. Quoted by McBride, ibid., 201.

## WORKS CONSULTED

Flynn, Thomas. *Sartre and Marxist Existentialism.* Chicago: University of Chicago Press, 1984.

Goldthorpe, Rhiannon. *Sartre: Literature and Theory.* Cambridge: Cambridge University Press, 1984.

McBride, William. *Sartre's Political Theory.* Bloomington: Indiana University Press, 1991.

Merleau-Ponty, Maurice. *Signs.* Trans. Richard McCleary. Evanston, Ill.: Northwestern University Press, 1964.

# 5

# Maurice Merleau-Ponty: Alterity and Dialogue

SHORTLY BEFORE HIS UNTIMELY DEATH in 1961, Merleau-Ponty commented on the present condition of philosophy, which he judged to be rendered, due to its reliance on "traditional means," "mute," paralyzed before "what the world is now living through." He characterized the dominant "Anglo–American analytic philosophy" as "a deliberate retreat into a universe of thought where contingency, ambiguity, and the concrete have no place" (TD 9). Western philosophy, in general, is dominated by a view of Being in which there "is not a trace of wavering," where "all visible properties result from a fundamental, sustaining infinity, a world in which clear reasons are developed for what appears initially to be a simple fact." While granting that "we owe much of what has engendered Western historical progress to it"— specifically, "the development of science" and " 'enlightenment' politics"—Merleau-Ponty advises that "it is also clear that this ontology is no longer justified in either our understanding or in our life" and that "by continuing to preserve it forcibly one cannot preserve what it once protected" (TD 11). Reading these words today, one cannot but notice their postmodern ring. These were not, in fact, thoughts that Merleau-Ponty had lately come upon, for his work began with the intention of undermining the mainstream traditions (empiricism and rationalism) of modernity. In *Phenomenology of Perception,* the sense of cultural crisis motivating his work occasionally breaks through the general sobriety of the book:

> Nature is *not* in itself geometrical, and it appears so only to a careful observer who contents himself with macrocosmic data. Human society is *not* a community of reasonable minds, and only in fortunate countries where a biological and economic balance has locally and temporarily been struck has such a conception of it been possible.

The experience of chaos, both on the speculative and the other level, prompts us to see rationalism in a historical perspective which it sets itself on principle to avoid, to seek a philosophy which explains the upsurge of reason in a world not of its own making and to prepare the substructure of living experience without which reason and liberty are emptied of their content and wither away. (PP 56–57)

Merleau-Ponty's "deconstruction" of modernity, it is important to note, was in no way to be a repudiation of "reason and liberty," but rather a project to reformulate them in terms of the "living experience" of the *doxa,* freed from the usual attempts to ground them in alleged necessary foundations. This is exemplified in remarks Merleau-Ponty made at a conference of artists, writers, and intellectuals from East and West in 1956, when he called for a "new universalism," one which "is no longer the universalism criticized under the name of 'bourgeois philosophy,' that is to say, an abstract reason that imagined one could, on the basis of principles truly common to all human beings and independent of all situations, pronounce truths and discover values" (TD 29). Invoking abstract principles implies, for Merleau-Ponty, a process of depersonalization, distancing us from "the social totality we live in." A universality based upon abstraction, which would be achieved by a transcendence of particularity in the sense of leaving it behind, is a false universality. For Merleau-Ponty, one cannot leave behind one's situatedness, and the attempt to do so will only result in the tragic consequence of mistaking the particular for the universal. Thus, while he claims allegiance to Husserl in the preface to *Phenomenology of Perception,* Merleau-Ponty is quick to separate himself from the former's quest for essences, the famous eidetic reduction through which phenomenology would find scientific status. Husserl's response to the crisis of European culture in the thirties was to proclaim that "the reason for the failure of rational culture . . . lies not in the essence of rationalism"[1] and to call for a renewed culture—"a new humanity"—founded upon the "supratemporal universality" opened by the phenomenological theory of essence. Merleau-Ponty's call for a "new universalism," in comparison, is clearly postmodern and is the outcome of the positions he took on such issues as body, speech, Others, and freedom in *Phenomenology of Perception*—positions which, I would argue, show him to be first and foremost a dialogical philosopher.

Recently, postmodern critics have raised questions about Merleau-Ponty's understanding of dialogue, questions that, by specifically addressing the issue of alterity in his thinking, jeopardize the authenticity of his critique of modernism and, with it, the project of his "new universalism." These critical questions are worthy, for in his opening remarks to *Phenomenology of Perception,* Merleau-Ponty, while situating himself within phenomenology, claims kinship both with Husserl and with phenomenology, prior to its self-conscious expression in Husserl's work, as "a style of thinking" common to such thinkers as Kierkegaard and Nietzsche. These comments, coming at the very first acquaintance of the reader with the text, have the effect of raising a question about the identity of the *Phenomenology of Perception,* a question that, we see, lingers after these many years. Is *Phenomenology of Perception* a work that continues, albeit creatively, the mainstream thought of Western philosophy (Husserl), or does it undermine and subvert that tradition (Kierkegaard and Nietzsche)? The issue of alterity, raised out of postmodern concerns, affords another opportunity to reopen the question of the identity of Merleau-Ponty's thought in *Phenomenology of Perception* and subsequent works dealing with alterity.

In his chapter on the *cogito* in *Phenomenology of Perception,* Merleau-Ponty aligns himself with a perspectivist theory of truth. There is first of all our species-perspective. He would seem to agree with Nietzsche, who claimed that we, as a species, "cannot look around our own corner" when he writes: "If I try to imagine Martians, or angels, or some divine thought outside the realm of my logic, this Martian, angelic or divine thought must figure in my universe without completely disrupting it. My thought, my self-evident truth is not one fact among others, but a value-fact which conditions every other possible one" (PP 398). All "necessary truths" are factual (species-contingent) and yet "necessary" in the sense that, for our species, they condition our type of thinking. When Merleau-Ponty went on to write that "if there had been no mankind with phonotory or articulatory organs, and a respiratory apparatus—or at least a body and the ability to move himself, there would have been no speech and no ideas" (PP 340–41), he is not suggesting that these facts are the occasion or material conditions for the discovery of an ideality that would contain a necessity independent of them: "every factual truth is a rational truth and *vice versa*" (PP 394). Continuing in this Nietzschean spirit, he goes on to claim that language plays the leading role in creating the myth of absolute or eternal truth. The "certainty which we enjoy of reaching beyond expression, a truth separable from it and of which expression is merely the garment and contingent manifestation, has been implanted in us by language" (PP 401). The table had been set for this view of truth in Merleau-Ponty's first book, *The Structure of Behavior,* in which he chose to criticize empiricism and behaviorism by positing "an a priori of the organism . . . the a priori of the species" (SB 123). What counts as a "stimulus" or an "excitant" is defined as such by the organism itself by virtue of its physiological constitution and vital interests: "It is the organism itself—according to the proper nature of its receptors, the thresholds of its nerve centers and the movements of the organs—which chooses the stimuli on the physical world to which it will be sensitive" (SB 13). This creates "a being for the animal" in the form of a specific "environment" for each species. It is against the background of this naturalism that Merleau-Ponty appropriates Husserl's notion of the "lifeworld" and phenomenological transcendentalism in *Phenomenology of Perception,* translating the species-environment correlation into that of subject-lifeworld.

The subject of the human lifeworld for Merleau-Ponty is a bodysubject in a practical, non-representational relationship to its environment, an "I can" instead of an "I think." The physiological species a priori subtends the functional subject as its condition of possibility, but Merleau-Ponty's emphasis from the start is on the functional development of the body, the body in action, the living body, wherein one's body is "the potentiality of a certain world" (PP 106). This living body "inhabits" its world outside of the traditional subject/object relationship. The bodysubject's functioning is understood holistically through the image of an "intentional arc," a weave of the physiological, biological, motor and sensory, and social and linguistic capacities of the bodysubject which are synthesized in action (save in pathological cases, which are the experiences closest to the empirical model). This holistic functioning is characterized by "ambiguity." Speaking of how the sexual pervades existence, he writes: "Sexuality is co-extensive with life. In other words, ambiguity is of the essence of human existence, and everything we live or think has always several meanings. . . . There is interfusion between sexuality and existence, which means that existence permeates sexuality and *vice versa,* so that it is impossible to determine, in a given decision or action, the proportion of sexual to other motivation, impossible to label a decision or act 'sexual' or 'non-sexual' " (PP 169). If for "sexual" are substituted such terms as "natural," "cultural," "linguistic," "perceptual," and so forth, one can see that, as ambiguity spreads out over existence, it would be impossible to preserve something called "the natural" or "the perceptual" from interfusion with the others. Rather, as Merleau-Ponty said, in the spirit of holism, "everything we live or think always has several meanings." It is against this background of what can be called "transcendental holism" that the question of alterity must be broached.

The problem of alterity appears in *Phenomenology of Perception* in terms of "the dilemma of the *for-itself* and *in-itself*" (PP 213). Merleau-Ponty defends the truth of the "for-itself," for "to have a body is to possess a universal setting, a schema of all types of perceptual unfolding" (PP 326). Thus, "the thing is correlative to my body and, in a more general terms, to my existence, of which my body is the stabilized structure. It is constituted in the hold my body takes upon it" (PP 320). ("Stabilized structure" here would include cultural assumptions.) Merleau-Ponty understands by "constitution" a dialogical process whereby, say, the perceiving body synergetically moves outside of itself in response to solicitation. In speaking of the blue of the sky, he writes in this vein: "Thus a sensible datum which is on the point of being felt sets a kind of muddled problem for my body to solve. I must find the right attitude which *will* provide it with the means of becoming determinate, of showing up as blue; I must find the reply to a question which is obscurely expressed. And yet I do so only when I am invited by it, my attitude is never sufficient to make me really see blue" (PP 214). In this "dialogue" or "transaction" between sensing and sensible, something determinate appears. A "thing" is an intersensory determinacy, the aim of "a bodily teleology" involving the body's synergic perceptual capacities. While the thing is the "corrolate" of the body's synergic capacities,

Merleau-Ponty insists that the thing appears as an "in-itself": "But the fact remains that the thing presents itself to the person who perceives it as a thing in itself, and thus poses the problem of a genuine *in-itself-for-us*." To bolster this contention and shore up the transcendence of the thing, Merleau-Ponty asserts that in our experience of the thing, "the thing holds itself aloof from us" (PP 322), the principal reason for which appears to be an appeal to "incompletion." The thing is always grasped perspectively, never given all at once, and is furthermore always embedded in a surrounding horizon with which it maintains relations. Neither the thing nor its worldly horizon is ever given in its total presence: "The thing and the world exist only insofar as they are experienced by me or subjects like me, since they are both the concatenation of our perspectives, yet they transcend all perspectives because this chain is temporal and incomplete" (PP 333).

The "transcendence" or alterity of Others is touched upon in the context of a discussion of solipsism, the customary threat to all transcendental philosophy. For Merleau-Ponty the existence of the Other is encountered "through the very first of all cultural objects, and the one by which all the rest exist . . . the body of the other person as the vehicle of a form of behavior" (PP 348). "A baby of fifteen months opens its mouth if I playfully take one of its fingers between my teeth and pretend to bite it." The reason for this is that "its mouth and teeth, as it feels them from the inside, are immediately, for it, an apparatus to bite with, and my jaw, as the baby sees it from the outside, is immediately, for it, capable of the same intentions. 'Biting' has immediately, for it, an intersubjective significance" (PP 352). It is as if, he says, both parties shared the same corporeal schema, or set of capacities, and that bodies, in their functioning, recognize one another in a non-representational manner. It is important to note that this bodily recognition of the existence of Others has its limits: "There is given the tension of my experience towards another whose existence on the horizon of my life is beyond doubt, even when my knowledge of him is imperfect" (PP 358). Language, dialogue, is called for, through which "common ground" is established and "coexistence" formed. But even in dialogue, I discover "an inexhaustible core" of another which is the very condition of dialogue and the irreducibility of the Other. Here, as with the transcendence of the thing, the reader of *Phenomenology of Perception* runs up against its central paradox of the in-itself-for-us: "The question is always how I can be open to phenomena which transcend me, and which nevertheless exist only to the extent that I take them up and live them; *how the presence to myself (Urpräsenz) which establishes my own limits and conditions every alien presence is at the same time depresentation (Entgegenwärtigung) and throws me outside of myself*" (PP 363).

Shortly after its publication, *Phenomenology of Perception* was the theme of a meeting of the Société Française de Philosophie. Merleau-Ponty delivered a brief presentation, summarizing the book's major theses and then opening himself to questions from members of the Société, which included Emile Brehier and Jean Hyppolite. His questioners were concerned with various aspects of his critiques of empiricism and rationalism and, in the main, defensive of those traditions. At the end of the session, Jean Beaufret came to Merleau-Ponty's support:

> I wish only to emphasize that many of the objections which have been addressed to Merleau-Ponty seem to me unjustified. I believe that they come down simply to objecting to his perspective itself, which is that of phenomenology. . . . Phenomenology is not a falling back into phenomenalism but the maintenance of contact with "the thing itself." If phenomenology rejects "intellectualist" explanations of perception, it is not to open the door to the irrational but to close it to verbalism. Nothing appears to me less pernicious than the *Phenomenology of Perception*. (PrP 41)

Then Beaufret interjects his own critical comments, quite different in their thrust from the other participants':

> The only reproach I would make to the author is not that he has gone "too far," but rather that he has not been sufficiently radical. The phenomenological descriptions which he uses in fact maintain the vocabulary of idealism. In this they are in accord with Husserlian descriptions. But the whole problem is precisely to know whether phenomenology, fully developed, does not require the abandonment of subjectivity and the vocabulary of subjective idealism. (PrP 41–42)

Merleau-Ponty, after many years, can be read as responding to Beaufret when he writes in his "Working Notes" of January 1959 in *The Visible and the Invisible* that his work in progress would "have to replace [the notions] of transcendental subjectivity, those of subject, object, meaning" (VI 167). One month later, he admits problems in *Phenomenology of Perception* due to its retention of "the philosophy of 'consciousness' " (VI 183). Beaufret was on the mark, for as Merleau-Ponty thought his project through he became convinced that his attempt to overcome modernity was caught in the very discourse of modernity. This intimately involved the issue of alterity.

Running throughout the "Working Notes" of *The Visible and the Invisible* are claims that *Erlebnis* (subjective experience) is to give way to the notion of *field:* "It is the Cartesian idealization applied to the mind as to the things (Husserl) that has persuaded us that we were a flux of individual *Erlebnisse,* whereas we are a field of Being" (VI 240). This shift marks the point where the "philosophy of consciousness" gives way to the new ontology proposed, quite schematically to be sure, in *The Visible and the Invisible.* By no means is Merleau-Ponty abandoning the notion of the subject or the importance of experience. This is clear from the opening sentence of the notes prepared for "Institution in Personal and Public History," included in *Themes from the Lectures at the Collège de France, 1952–1960,* where he writes that "the concept of institution may help us to find a solution to certain difficulties in the philosophy of consciousness" (TL 39). Specifically, he suggests that "if the subject were taken not as a constituting but an instituting subject, it might be understood that the subject does not exist instantaneously and that the other person does not exist as a negative of myself" (TL 39, 40). By "institution" he means "those events in experience which endow it with durable dimensions in relation to which a whole series of other experiences will acquire meaning, will form an intelligible series or a history" (TL 40). The temporality of the instituting subject is the concrete temporality of a tradition or specific history, a hermeneutic temporality, not the abstract temporality of the temporal phases of an individual consciousness as in phenomenology. The instituting subject shares a tradition with others, the tradition serving as a "hinge" of experiences. The ontology being worked out in *The Visible and the Invisible* evolves from the notion of institution. Being, in this new ontology, "is staggered out in depth," that is, is a tissue of fields, regions, dimensions, and levels, both sensuous and ideal. In *Phenomenology of Perception,* the sensuous and ideal were elements in the "intentional arc" of the subject itself, retaining the modern notion of the a priori and constitution. In *The Visible and the Invisible,* he claims that "the transcendental field is a field of transcendencies. The transcendental . . . *goes beyond the subjectivity"* (VI 172). The "categories" conceived to be transcendentally subjective in a "philosophy of consciousness" now are considered to be "transcendent," not issuing from a subjectivity which would then apply them constitutively. "Being is the 'place' where the 'modes of consciousness' are inscribed as structurations of Being (a way of thinking oneself within a society is implied in its social structure), and where the structurations of Being are modes of consciousness" (VI 353). The "anonymous" is no longer a dimension of subjectivity, but the level where a subject is inscribed, "held," with Others, by Being itself:

> With the first vision, the first contact, the first pleasure, there is intuition, that is, not the positing of a content, but the opening of a dimension that can never again closed, the establishment of a level in terms of which every other experience will henceforth be situated. The idea is this level, this dimension. It is therefore not a *de facto* invisible, like an object hidden behind another, and not an absolute invisible, which would have nothing to do with the visible. Rather it is the invisible *of* this world, that which inhabits this world, sustains it, and renders it visible, its own and interior possibility, the Being of this being. (VI 151)

The discourse of institution, of field, level, and dimension, has its roots in structuralism, which stressed the productive power of various structures (discourses primarily) to generate experience and intelligibility. Merleau-Ponty admits sensuous fields, such as color and sound, into the play of production, a play in which these sensuous fields overlap with other fields in the production of language, perception, painting, and music, which themselves continuously produce experience. And unlike a certain tendency in structuralist literature, Merleau-Ponty, as noted, retains the notion of the subject, for he remains, if not quite a phenomenologist, a philosopher of experience. There are fields of experience, but all experience implies a certain distance, which Merleau-Ponty conceives of as *écart*, in opposition to Sartre's notion of *néant*. *Néant* marks a break with Being, an introduction of incommensurability, as evident in Sartre's claim that the body's "double sensations," in which it, for example, touches itself, create "two essentially different orders of reality . . . two incommensurable levels . . . which it is useless to try to unite."[2] Merleau-Ponty's *écart* is a distance *within Being*, as is evident, he argues, when the body touches itself, for the arm that touches is itself tangible. Experience precludes the fusion of immediacy: "If I express this experience by saying that the things are in their place and that we fuse with them, I immediately make the experience itself impossible" (VI 122). Experience requires a subjectivity carved out by difference, a difference which is productive of meaning, what Merleau-Ponty calls "a privative non-coinciding, a coinciding from afar, a divergence, and something like a 'good error' . . . a distance which is not the contrary of proximity" (VI 125). This is true for sensuous and ideal experience: "The thickness of flesh between the seer and the thing is constitutive for the thing of its visibility as for the seer of his corporeity; it is not an obstacle between them, it is their means of communication" (VI 135). Language is not a screen that separates us from things and from gaining some original experience of them, but is rather "the life of things" by being a dimension of the "infrastructure" of experience. All experience is imbued with dimensions and levels, of the sensuous (space, color, sound, etc.) and of the ideal (symbols, language, traditions, etc.). The experiencing subject is the place where these dimensions and levels "coil up" on themselves. The subject is both instituted and instituting insofar as it both finds itself contingently installed in these dimensions and levels and is compelled to carry them on in future experience, action, expression, and communication.

*Écart* introduces Merleau-Ponty's revised thinking about alterity. On one occasion he refers to the "syntax" of Being, and on another, with reference to Lacan, to a vision and thought which are "structured as a language" (VI 83, 126). Being itself, we have noted, is structured in the form of various levels or dimensions of the sensuous and ideal which are productive of meaning. The manner of this productivity is diacritical opposition. The move from *Erlebnisse* to *Urstiftung* implies that "the 'objects' of consciousness themselves are not something positive *in front of* us" (VI 238–39). Words in discourse "mean" in terms of their divergent relationships among themselves. This is true as well, Merleau-Ponty points out, for perceptual meanings, which are no longer viewed as arising through a process of constitution, but rather through a process of "segregation": "I describe perception as a diacritical, relative, oppositional system" (VI 213). Color is a dimension according to which one perceives, and a specific color is a variant within this dimension. A specific red "is not a chunk of absolutely hard, indivisible being . . . but rather a sort of straits between exterior horizons and interior horizons . . . a certain differentiation . . . less a color or a thing, therefore, than a difference between things and colors" (VI 132). While most of *The Visible and the Invisible* is more suggestive than worked out, it is clear that Merleau-Ponty was framing the issue of alterity in terms of "institution" (structures) instead of "constitution." In *Phenomenology of Perception,* alterity (transcendence) appeared in terms of the "paradox" of his transcendentalism, how what is Other can appear as such within the terms of the intentional arc, the paradoxical in–itself–for–us. In *The Visible and the Invisible,* he clearly moves the problem to new ground with the announcement that "it is indeed a paradox of Being, not a paradox of man, that we are dealing with here" (VI 136). Against a transcendentalism such as Sartre's, which attributes all "determinations" to the negating function of consciousness, Merleau-Ponty contrasts his "institutional" approach: "This *separation* (*écart*) which, in first approximation, forms meaning, is not a no I affect *myself* with, a lack which I constitute as a lack by the upsurge of an *end* which I give myself—it is a *natural* negativity, a first institution, always already there" (VI 217). In place of the in–itself–for–us one finds that "transcendence is identity within difference"; regarding the Same and Other: "What do I bring to the problem of the same and the other? This: that the same be the other than the other, and identity difference of difference" (VI 225, 264). In this new context, the Other is no more problematic than the Same (the self). Identity does not "hold" by itself, so the Same and the Other implicate one another: "There is not identity, nor non–identity, or non-coincidence, there is inside and outside turning about one another" (VI 264).

While acknowledging "the powerful originality of Merleau-Ponty's work," Emmanuel Levinas judges that it remains committed to a phenomenology which, though revised in an interesting way—from "I think" to "I can"—nonetheless amounts to a reduction of the Other to the Same. From Levinas's perspective, Merleau-Ponty's bodysubject continues the tradition of transcendental gnosis, through which the Other is converted into the state of "phenomenon" and falls into the grasp of a subject, albeit a bodysubject with a practical grasp of phenomena. He notes that for Merleau-Ponty "it is the incarnate subject which, in assembling being, will raise the curtain."[3] Besides noting this body-conditioning of experience, Levinas points out that the body's power of conditioning, for Merleau-Ponty, is extended through the sedimentation of culture, of language, to form an always present "horizon" of experience. Merleau-Ponty comes—along with such philosophers as Hegel, with his rational totality, Husserl, with his transcendental egology, and Heidegger, with his encompassing Being—to bear the brunt of Levinas's persistent and vigorous effort to defend the Other from reduction to the Same. These thinkers, in Levinas's estimation, repeat the traditional Western tendency to reduce alterity. "Western philosophy," he writes, "coincides with the disclosure of the other, where the other, in manifesting itself as a being, loses its alterity. From infancy philosophy has been struck with a horror of the other that remains other—with an insurmountable allergy."[4] Metaphysics, as the "first" or "highest" expression of philosophy, gathers into its reach, without any secrets, all that is, reducing reality to cognition. This cognitive totalitarianism is unacceptable to Levinas. "The other," he tells us, "is other than Being. Being excludes all alterity."[5]

It would indeed appear that Merleau-Ponty's deepest, and anti-dualist, intuitions, reflected in the bodysubject, gestalt, inter-world, flesh, and reversibility, are quite antithetical to Levinas's sharp dichotomies—metaphysics/ethics, True/Good, narcissism/substitution. Yet, as we have observed, Merleau-Ponty himself was concerned with preserving alterity. In *Phenomenology of Perception*, he invokes the notion of "infinity" in defense of transcendence when he claims that "perception entails a process of making explicit which could be pursued to infinity" (PP 343). An explicit thematic figure always appears on a background which "runs off" in many directions. An attempt to thematize the background will only serve to constitute another figure/background situation entailing the same difficulty. This notion of the transcendent as "infinity" in the sense of "absence" is not acceptable to Levinas, for whom the transcendent Other is "an absence not reducible to hiddenness."[6] While, in *Phenomenology of Perception,* Merleau-Ponty disclaims the rationalist tradition's pretention to a full grasp of the Other in favor of a perspectival grasp, Levinas would preserve the Other from all grasp, and seek a notion of the Other as a "positive" infinite. Merleau-Ponty himself, as we have shown, was unsatisfied with his understanding of transcendence/ alterity in the "philosophy of consciousness" approach of *Phenomenology of Perception* and went on to develop, in *The Visible and the Invisible,* an understanding of alterity as integral to Being: "If coincidence is lost, this is no accident; if Being is hidden, this is itself a characteristic of Being, and no disclosure will make us comprehend it" (VI 122). Transcendence/alterity here is not constituted by the perceiver's own finitude, but is the condition of any "presence," any positive identity whatsoever. Merleau-Ponty clearly refuses an ontology which conceives of Being in terms of a collection of positive entities. On the other hand, he is opposed to the notion of a difference as *néant* in Sartre's philosophy, an otherness than Being, beyond Being. Merleau-Ponty is a philosopher who finds alterity in the lifeworld, appearances, the *doxa.* His ontology directly challenges Levinas's contention that "being excludes alterity."

Levinas's critique of ontology is tied to his fundamental concern for ethics. He sees, as an ethicist, in the totalizing tendencies of ontology an attitude translatable into totalitarianism. To counter this, the Other must be delivered from the clutches of cognition and restored to its rightful place in the ethical "face to face" relations which comprise "sociality." Merleau-Ponty did not write about "ethics" as such, but did address the social in a way that makes it possible to find a certain ethical dimension in his thinking. His social and ethical thinking relate directly to his concern for alterity and will allow for further comparison with

Levinas, specifically, the latter's "face to face" relation and the former's dialogical relation.

Already in *Phenomenology of Perception* it was possible to see the dialogical relation in Merleau-Ponty's thinking. Perception itself is considered as "a sort of dialogue" between the synergic body and the world, but the dialogic relationship between interlocutors is of pivotal importance, for it is through dialogue that there emerges the possibility of becoming aware of and transgressing the limits of one's own perspective. For our purposes the following text from *Phenomenology of Perception* is quite revealing:

> In the experience of dialogue, there is constituted between the other person and myself a common ground; my thought and his are interwoven into a single fabric, my words and those of my interlocutor are called forth by the state of the discussion, and they are inserted into a shared operation of which neither of us is the creator. We have here a dual being where the Other is no longer for me a bit of behavior in my transcendental field, nor I in his. We are collaborators in a consummate reciprocity. Our perspectives merge into each other, and we coexist through a common world. In the present dialogue, I am freed from myself, for the Other person's words are certainly his; they are not of my own making, though I do grasp them the moment they come into being, or even anticipate them. And indeed, the objection which my interlocutor raises to what I say draws from me thoughts which I had no idea I possessed, so that at the same time that I lend him thoughts, he reciprocates by making me think too. (PP 354)

Notice how the dialogical experience is a decentering experience, what Gabriel Marcel calls an "anti-Copernican" experience. "I am," Merleau-Ponty says, "freed from myself." The subject/object relationship characteristic of cognition is transcended, for there is created a "dual being," a "shared operation," a "reciprocity." Not only do I meet the limits of my perspective, but the Other enables me "by making me think," and the idea of universality arises. Most importantly for our purposes, there is the acknowledgment of the ethical dimension of the communicative situation when Merleau-Ponty sees that "the other is for me no longer a bit of behavior in my transcendental field, nor I in his." In dialogue a special coexistence is born in which the participants are in an I/Thou relationship. The master/slave relation has no place. Interlocutors are "collaborators," and each "lends" to and "draws" from the other.

The notion of dialogue comes to the fore in works subsequent to *Phenomenology of Perception,* such as *Signs* and *Adventures of the Dialectic.* These works are, in my estimation, very congenial with the ontology of *The Visible and the Invisible,* which rejects essences as well as "the return to the immediate, the coincidence, the effective fusion with the existent, the search for an original integrity, for a secret lost and to be rediscovered, which would nullify our questions" (VI 122). The *écart,* or distance at the core of the "doubling" formative of subjectivity, requires that all experience and thought be interpretation, since they must be "inscribed in the order of being" that they disclose. A fine example of this is found in *Signs,* in "Indirect Language and the Voices of Silence," dedicated to Sartre, and a reply to his "What Is Literature?" Sartre used this work as the occasion to propose a sketch of authentic human relationships, in contrast with the inauthentic and conflictual relationships traced out in *Being and Nothingness.* Merleau-Ponty opposes Sartre's analysis in several important ways, but overall his purpose is, like Sartre's, to feature reciprocity. For Merleau-Ponty, all language use takes place in a community, a space of exchange structured by fields such as art, religion, and law. Communication always involves a "response" on the part of a speaker or artist insofar as he or she takes up a field in the form of a tradition which "suggests," "invites" response, "outlines a future." Meaning does not originate in the "mind" of the speaker or artist, but is found as sketched out in the fields of meaning to which they belong. In phenomena of expression, the individual, for Merleau-Ponty, inevitably deviates, "transgresses" fields of meaning, constantly modifying them in contingent circumstances and addressing him- or herself to others by the sedimentation of oneself in fields available to others. To express oneself is "a response to what the world, the past, and the completed works demanded. It is accomplishment and brotherhood" (S 59). One is always already installed in expressive life as a "perpetual conversation woven together by all speech, all valid works and actions, each according to its place and circumstance, contesting and confirming the other, each one re-creating all the others." According to Merleau-Ponty, "speech . . . contains its own . . . ethics" (S 77) insofar as language "is a *call* which situated thought addresses to other thoughts equally situated, and each one responds to the call with its own resources" (PrP 8). In communicative exchanges, both within a certain field (such as painting, or even impressionist painting) and across fields, whether interdisciplinary or intercultural, "the other to whom I address myself and I who express myself are incontestably linked together. . . . The other whom I respect gets his life from me as I get mine from him" (S 73). The Other is grasped as deserving of respect in the very process through which I address him or her, and it is likewise with myself.

Levinas's understanding of sociality revolves around what he calls the "face to face" relationship, a relationship which, he insists, eludes the "grasp" or prehension characteristic of cognitive phenomena. The face is not, for Levinas, a "phenomenon," and he would resist Merleau-Ponty's claim that "to see a face is to take a certain hold upon it" (PP 252). To consider the face as a phenomenon is to subject it to totalization and deny its ethical transcendence. The "face to face" relation occurs in language, but is not reducible to language. In order to sustain the claim that the Other is not a phenomenon, Levinas distinguishes between "saying" (*Dire*) and "said" (*Dit*). Saying is the performative act of "exposure" and "approach" at the basis of all communication. Saying has its own way of signifying, which is ethical, whereas the said signifies phenomenologically or ontologically as the truth. In exposing him- or herself to me in salutation or address, the Other stops the intentional thrust of my meaning-giving or context-situating acts, imposing a limit upon me, subjecting me to the Other. "You shall not commit murder" is inscribed on a face and constitutes its alterity, its transcendence of all transcendental or ontological categories of meaning. In my subjection I find myself responsible for the Other, an ethical "hostage" to the Other, not in a relationship of reciprocity, but in a relation where the Other is superior. Saying, as presentation of the Good, is, for Levinas, prior to and irreversible with the said as the realm of the True. Levinas's insistence on the separation between ethics and ontology is reflected in his comments on the phenomenon of reversibility: "The reversibility of a relation where the terms are indifferently read from left to right and from right to left would couple them *one* to the *other*. . . . The intended transcendence would be thus absorbed into the unity of the system, destroying the radical alterity of the Other."[7] Merleau-Ponty's ontology, however, resists absorbing differences, which are built into Being as we have seen. It is true that Merleau-Ponty claimed that "reversibility . . . is the ultimate truth" (VI 135), but his understanding of reversibility is not reductive. Being, for him, is not a systematic gathering of positive entities, nor does it involve a reduction of multiplicitous terms to the same. Reversibility signifies rather the style (flesh) or way it is with Being which allows terms to circulate, overlap, encroach upon one another in various relationships without coinciding.

An instance of reversibility would be the dialogical relationship, which honors alterity, without which dialogue would not be what it is, while recognizing the interlocutors' common participation in the process itself. Both Levinas and Merleau-Ponty respect alterity and regard the ethical irreducibility of the Other, but in quite different ways. While Levinas is suspicious of the leveling effect of ontologies, especially as they have been traditionally realized, and would remove the Other altogether from ontology, Merleau-Ponty is suspicious of attempts to surpass the lifeworld, appearances, *doxa,* especially as they have been traditionally realized. Just as for Merleau-Ponty "pure thought" cannot mean save by coming into words and into the world, so also for him a "pure command" would oblige only by reference to a specific situation calling for an appropriate response. Perhaps one could say, for Merleau-Ponty did not, that ethics is a dimension of Being which, while unique in its difference from other dimensions, overlaps other dimensions. This would not reduce ethics to ontology, but intertwine it with other experiences. Levinas, in fact, once made a remark in which one finds this echoed. He referred to the problem of how one can both comprehend the Other as an object and speak to the Other as an interlocutor, how, in other words, one grasps the Other in the context of the world and also addresses the irreducible ethical Other: "The Other is not an object of comprehension first and an interlocutor second. The two relations are *intertwined.* In other words, the comprehension of the Other is inseparable from his or her invocation."[8] Levinas's recognition of an "intertwining" between the ethical and the situational or worldly, as well as Merleau-Ponty's characterization of language as a "call," present a promising point of intersection of their works for a positive rapprochement.

Merleau-Ponty's understanding of alterity has been criticized from another direction by some feminist philosophers. In a recent article in *Hypatia,* Shannon Sullivan recapitulates much of this criticism, while giving it a focus that has a direct impact upon our account of Merleau-Ponty as a dialogical thinker. She begins by noting that, while appreciating Merleau-Ponty's emphasis upon the body, "feminist philosophers have noted that in his work the body has no gender and that, as a result, his account of embodied existence is not neutral, but androcentric."[9] Due to his unconsciousness of the implications of sexual difference, Merleau-Ponty is unaware that he speaks from it in a non-neutral and biased fashion. In fact, Sullivan points out, it is not just sexual difference that goes unrecognized in his work, but differences of "class, race, age, culture, nationality, individual experiences and upbringing, and more," so that "Merleau-Ponty's intersubjective dialogue often turns out to be a solipsistic subject's monologue that includes elimination of others in its very 'communication' with them. Because the particularities of bodies have been overlooked, Merleau-Ponty's account of subjectivity is built upon the domination of others."[10] Traditionally, philosophers have cited "an essential 'core' in humans that underlies all of their cultural (and other) differences,"[11] such as "Reason," "Universal Mind," and "Transcendental Ego." Merleau-Ponty differs "merely by locating this fundamental core in the body," so that all individual bodies share a sameness which is then "overlaid by the differences that our particularities give them."[12] With regard to my question as to whether *Phenomenology of Perception* continues with the tradition or marks a subversion of it, Sullivan judges that the former is clearly the case.

Sullivan establishes her critique by citing Merleau-Ponty's use of "anonymous" and "impersonal" to depict body intentionality, as he does specifically to ensure intercorporeality and avoid solipsism. In this context he holds that "my body and the other's are one whole, two sides of the same phenomenon, and the anonymous existence of which my body is the ever renewed trace henceforth inhabits both bodies simultaneously" (PP 354). The very terms "anonymous" and "impersonal," Sullivan argues, imply that on a basic level there are no differences among bodies, that differences will enter at some later time. If the Other's body is in this way, as Merleau-Ponty puts it, "a miraculous prolongation of my own intentions" (PP 354), then I have a sure entry into understanding the Other. But because for Sullivan differences reach all the way down, and Merleau-Ponty does not see this, his anonymous understanding of Others in terms of "prolongation" is an imposition and domination of Others, a refusal to recognize differences and, of course, another unfortunate case of mistaking the universal for the particular.

Sullivan's reading of *Phenomenology of Perception* echoes Judith Butler's and Jacques Derrida's insofar as Sullivan finds there an "anonymous" body, Butler a "natural" body, and Derrida a "perception," all untouched by difference. These readings have a textual basis in Merleau-Ponty's claim to be carrying on Husserl's notion of the "primacy of perception," a vestige of modern empiricism. Indeed, Merleau-Ponty takes up the founding-founded distinction of that tradition, lending credibility to charges that he is laying differences on some primordial level of sameness, that there is a foundational "pretext" of an elaborated world. This being given, Sullivan chooses to discount the tensions in *Phenomenology of Perception,* the texts which strain against the tradition. (For an example of a reading of *Phenomenology of Perception* as a subversive text, see Gary Madison's "Did Merleau-Ponty Have a Theory of Perception?")[13] We have noted the notion of ambiguity, wherein "everything we live or think has always several meanings." The "projective" function of Merleau-Ponty's transcendentalism, the intentional arc, includes past experiences, sexuality, language, the symbolic—dimensions that are not self-contained, but which spread into one another—which leads him to conclude that "it is impossible to superimpose on man a lower layer of behavior which one chooses to call 'natural,' followed by a manufactured cultural or spiritual world. Everything is both manufactured and natural in man" (PP 189). This is why Merleau-Ponty can refer to the body as "the very first of all cultural objects, and the one by which all the rest exist," and yet also describe the body as a "natural self." The way that the various levels of the intentional arc "spread" into one another is articulated in terms of the founding-founded relationship which, although he struggles to control it for his purposes, will have for readers such as Sullivan too many traces of the tradition.

> The relation of reason to fact, or eternity to time, like that of reflection to the unreflective, of thought to language or of thought to perception is the two-way relationship that phenomenology has called *Fundierung;* the founding term, or originator—time, the unreflective, the fact, language, perception—is primary in the sense that the originated is presented as a determinate or explicit form of the originator, which prevents the latter from reabsorbing the former, and yet the originator is not primary in the empiricist sense and the originated is not simply derived, since it is through the originated that the originator is made manifest. (PP 394)

The building model, employing levels on levels, with the claim that the "originated" is "a determinate or explicit form of the originator," legitimates the traditional reading, while the reservation that "the originator is not primary in the empiricist sense and the originated is not simply derived" legitimates the subversive reading. Applied to sexuality, one can, in the spirit of a subversive reading, hold that there is no sexual originary untouched by differences and that there are many ways to be sexual. While I think that this is a valid way to read the meaning of sexuality in *Phenomenology of Perception,* I would agree with Sullivan and other feminist critics that Merleau-Ponty's phenomenological descriptions of sexuality are gender-biased and that there is a tension between his assertions about the ambiguity of sexuality and his unconsciousness of his own gendered sexuality. Merleau-Ponty became, as we have seen, increasingly aware of the shortcomings of *Phenomenology of Perception* and of how he was trapped to a certain extent in the very discourse he was trying to overcome. In *The Visible and the Invisible* he wrote that "there is no hierarchy of orders or layers or planes (VI 270). He resisted images of layering with the image of circularity: "There is no longer the originating and the derived; there is a thought traveling a circle where the condition and the conditioned, the reflection and the reflected, are in a reciprocal relationship, and *where the end is in the beginning as much as the beginning is in the end*" (VI 35; emphasis added). Yet, Sullivan argues that Merleau-Ponty's ontology only ensconces him further in a "dominating" dialogue.

Merleau-Ponty has moved in his ontology, Sullivan acknowledges, "from the phenomenological explanation of corporeal communication presented in *Phenomenology of Perception* to an ontological account of the condition of possibility of corporeal communication: the presence of the subject and its world for each other."[14] She appreciates that *The Visible and the Invisible* recognizes the *écart* or difference required for all communication and production of meaning, but claims that Merleau-Ponty loses all that is of worth in his discussion of communication by melting it into an ontological sameness of Being in "flesh": "By moving from the ontic to the ontological, the topic of discussion for Merleau-Ponty is no longer individual beings but Being, which— since it is neither a being nor a group of beings nor a description of the general characteristics of beings—tells us very little about the concrete, practical ways in which beings live and thus in no way contributes to an understanding of how dialogue with one another might be made possible."[15] Merleau-Ponty's later work "answers our ontic question of how subject and object are different and yet can understand or communicate with one another with the ontological claim that behind our differences lies a sameness—the flesh—that we are."[16] My own view is that the ontology of *The Visible and the Invisible* is precisely the result of Merleau-Ponty's thinking about issues of sociality and communication and expresses a non-reductive multiplicity of perspectives that communicate without losing distinctness. The ontology has its roots, as pointed out previously, in his course outline "Institution in Personal and Public History," which offers criticism of phenomenology (philosophy of consciousness) in the light of experiences of "coexistence." More precisely, the ontology reflects the growing hermeneutical dimension of Merleau-Ponty's thinking apparent especially in his essays on philosophy and social science.

In his essay "The Philosopher and Sociology," Merleau-Ponty criticizes the assumption by traditional philosophers of an unconditioned thought. One begins to think from situatedness: "Whatever truth we may have is to be gotten not in spite of but through our historical inherence. . . . [M]y contact with the social in the finitude of my situation is revealed to me as the point of origin of all truth" (S 109). In *Phenomenology of Perception,* Merleau-Ponty had argued that thought is linguistic. He now amplifies: thinking is thoroughly social. The philosopher's ideas and certainties are "caught up . . . in the fabric of the culture he belongs to, they cannot be truly known by just being scrutinized and varied in thought, but must be confronted with other cultural formations and viewed against the background of preconceptions" (S 108). The words "varied in thought" refer to Husserl's method of reaching a universal essence by means of imaginary variation of examples, as though the contingencies of historical experience were somehow contained within the scope of the philosopher's imagination. Immersion in history, Merleau-Ponty rejoins, "prohibits the philosopher from arrogating to himself an immediate access to the universal" (S 109). He proposes in his essay "From Mauss to Claude Lévi-Strauss" a different conception of the universal, "no longer the overarching universal of a strictly objective method, but a sort of lateral universal which we acquire through ethnological experience and its incessant testing of the self through the other person and the other person through the self" (S 120). Moreover, "the equipment of our social being can be dismantled and reconstructed by the voyage" (S 119). The very categories of our thinking are embedded in our cultural/historical way of life. Encounter with other points of view allows us to become aware of our categories, test their comprehensive capacities, and modify or reconstruct them. This is "rationality in contingency" wherein there is neither a total nor an immediate guarantee. "It is somehow open, which is to say that it is menaced" (PrP 23). In his *Adventures of the Dialectic,* Merleau-Ponty attempts to display the "echoes" and overlap between politics and ethnological experience. Traditional liberalism presumed a given unity, a realized universal in an existent "humanity" which transcended inessential differences. Marxism, as well, assumed the universal in the form of the proletariat. Both proved liable to mistaking the universal for the particular. Merleau-Ponty calls for a "new liberalism which no longer believes in "universal harmony," which "legitimizes its adversaries," and which "conceives itself as a task" (AD 7). The new liberalism expresses the lateral universal, the contingent nature of one's truths, the multiplicity of perspectives, the creation of common ground, the inevitable openness of meaning. The new liberalism is based on a conception of dialogue where one's views are "incomplete so long as they do not pass into other perspectives and into the perspectives of others. Nothing is more foreign to it than the Kantian conception of an ideality of the world which is the same in everyone, just as the number two or the triangle is the same in mind, outside of meetings or exchanges" (AD 204). In all dialogue, as in anthropological studies, Merleau-Ponty insists, one must establish a "ground where we [the interlocutors] shall both be intelligible without any reduction or rash transposition" (S 122). The force of these texts I have been citing shows beyond any doubt Merleau-Ponty's full commitment to dialogue, a notion that runs even deeper and more extensively in his later works. His acceptance of, even respect for, differences is apparent in the sensitivity he expresses for the finitude and contingencies of one's own views, and how they, while inevitable starting points, can themselves be sources of misunderstanding and require reconstruction.

We have observed how Merleau-Ponty found overlap between his reflections on philosophy, the social sciences, and politics in the form of his proposal for a new liberalism. The ontology of *The Visible and the Invisible,* while apparently so different from his essays on the social sciences and politics because lacking explicit reference to them, maintains, for me, implied reference. *The Visible and the Invisible* does not separate ontic and ontological, as if what Merleau-Ponty had discovered in his writings on the social sciences and politics were simply ontic and had no ontological relevance. His ontology is an ontology of the lifeworld, appearances, the *doxa.* Being is the tissue or fabric of the sensuous and ideal levels through which our concrete experience holds together and makes sense. What the ontology is meant to reveal about the lifeworld is precisely what Merleau-Ponty had discovered about communicative processes, and that is the inevitable existence of differences, multiplicity of points of view, the inherent ambiguous, interpretative dimension of all experience. Flesh "brings a style of being wherever there is a fragment of being" (VI 139); that is, flesh is the "way it is" with Being, a weaving of difference and encroachment. Flesh is similarity, not sameness, for it includes difference. The ontology expresses the weave of difference and encroachment that runs throughout Merleau-Ponty's writings on sociology and ethnology, where he speaks of various cultures as "different crystallizations of an initial polymorphism of the body as vehicle of being-in-the-world" (S 101). Culturally different bodies are not the same bodies, for to call them the same would exclude the social and psychological "techniques of the body" (S 101) which culturally differentiate them. He refers to cultures as "variants," but not in the sense of variants of the same. Culture does not deliver us from nature so that cultures are equivocal or incommensurate. Rather, nature is always found to be culturally differenced. To use classical terminology (which Merleau-Ponty did not), humanity is neither univocally the same nor equivocally different, but analogically similar. (He often uses the Wittgensteinian "family resemblances" to express what he means by similarity and kinship.)

While Sullivan sees an intractable insensitivity to alterity in both *Phenomenology of Perception* and *The Visible and the Invisible,* and a consequent distorted view of dialogue, I see the former work as in tension with itself over the question of alterity but by no means exhibiting an unambiguous solipsism or "ventriloquism," and the latter work as an ontology elaborated to award place to alterity and sustain dialogical coexistence. We began our reflections on Merleau-Ponty and alterity with some comments he made in an interview with Madaleine Chapsal shortly before his death in which he expressed sentiments about the failure of traditional Western philosophy to speak to contemporary issues because of its devaluation of "contingency, ambiguity, and the concrete" (what postmodernism would call the local) and its penchant for totalizing explanations (what postmodernism would call metanarratives). Such metaphysics "is no longer justified." He praises Western progress in the form of " 'enlightenment' politics," but the thrust of his comments severs it from its traditional foundations. It is possible to see Merleau-Ponty's own "new liberalism" and ontology of the flesh as attempts to politically and ontologically reconstruct the tradition.


### WORKS OF MERLEAU-PONTY CITED

AD     *Adventures of the Dialectic.* Trans. Joseph Bien. Evanston, Ill.: Northwestern University Press, 1973 (*Les Aventures de la dialectique.* Paris: Gallimard, 1955).

PP       *Phenomenology of Perception.* Trans. Colin Smith. New
         York: Humanities Press, 1962 (*Phénoménologie de la percep-
         tion.* Paris: Gallimard, 1945).
PrP      *The Primacy of Perception and Other Essays.* Ed. James Edie.
         Evanston, Ill.: Northwestern University Press, 1964 (con-
         tains the cited essays "An Unpublished Text," trans. Ar-
         leen Dallery, and "The Primacy of Perception and Its
         Philosophical Consequences," trans. James Edie).
S        *Signs.* Trans. Richard McCleary. Evanston, Ill.: North-
         western University Press, 1964 (contains the cited essays
         "Indirect Language and the Voices of Silence," "The
         Philosopher and Sociology," and "From Mauss to Lévi-
         Strauss") (*Signes.* Paris: Gallimard, 1960).
SB       *The Structure of Behavior.* Trans. Alden Fisher. Boston:
         Beacon Press, 1963 (*La Structure du comportement.* Paris:
         Presses Universitaires de France, 1942).
TD       *Texts and Dialogues on Philosophy, Politics, and Culture.* Ed.
         Hugh J. Silverman and James Barry, Jr. Trans. Michael
         Smith et al. Atlantic Highlands, N.J.: Humanities Press,
         1992 (contains the cited works "Merleau-Ponty in Per-
         son: An Interview with Madeleine Chapsal" and "East-
         West Encounter").
TL       *Themes from the Lectures at the Collège de France, 1952–
         1960.* Trans. John O'Neill. Evanston, Ill.: Northwestern
         University Press, 1970. (*Résumés de cours: Collège de
         France, 1952–1960.* Paris: Gallimard, 1960).
VI       *The Visible and the Invisible.* Trans. Alphonso Lingis. Ev-
         anston, Ill.: Northwestern University Press, 1968 (*Le Vis-
         ible et l'invisible.* Paris: Gallimard, 1964).

## NOTES

1. Edmund Husserl, *The Crisis of European Sciences and Transcendental Phenomenology,* trans. David Carr (Evanston, Ill.: Northwestern University Press, 1970), 299.

2. Jean-Paul Sartre, *Being and Nothingness,* trans. Hazel Barnes (New York: Philosophical Library, 1956), 402.

3. Emmanuel Levinas, "Meaning and Sense," in *Collected Philosophi-*

*cal Papers,* trans. Alphonso Lingis (The Hague: Martinus Nijhoff, 1987), 80.

4. Emmanuel Levinas, "The Trace of the Other," in *Deconstruction in Context,* ed. Mark Taylor, trans. Alphonso Lingis (Chicago: University of Chicago Press, 1986), 346.

5. Emmanuel Levinas, "Philosophy and the Idea of Infinity," in *Collected Philosophical Papers,* 70.

6. Levinas, "Trace of the Other," 347.

7. Emmanuel Levinas, *Totality and Infinity,* trans. Alphonso Lingis (Pittsburgh: Duquesne University Press, 1969), 35.

8. Emmanuel Levinas, "Is Ontology Fundamental?" trans. Peter Atterton, *Philosophy Today,* Summer 1989, 125.

9. Shannon Sullivan, "Domination and Dialogue in Merleau-Ponty's *Phenomenology of Perception,*" *Hypatia* 12 (Winter 1997): 1.

10. Ibid.

11. Ibid., 7.

12. Ibid., 8.

13. Gary Madison, "Did Merleau-Ponty Have a Theory of Perception?" in *Merleau-Ponty, Hermeneutics, and Postmodernism,* ed. Thomas W. Busch and Shaun Gallagher (Albany: State University of New York Press, 1992), 83–106.

14. Sullivan, "Domination and Dialogue," 14.

15. Ibid., 15.

16. Ibid., 14.

## Works Consulted

Dillon, M. C. *Merleau-Ponty's Ontology.* Bloomington: Indiana University Press, 1988.

Husserl, Edmund. *The Crisis of European Sciences and Transcendental Phenomenology.* Trans. David Carr. Evanston: Northwestern University Press, 1970.

Levinas, Emmanuel. *Collected Philosophical Papers.* Trans. Alphonso Lingis. The Hague: Martinus Nijhoff, 1987.

———. *Totality and Infinity.* Trans. Alphonso Lingis. Pittsburgh: Duquesne University Press, 1969.

———. "The Trace of the Other." In *Deconstruction in Context,* ed. Mark Taylor, trans. Alphonso Lingis, 345–59. Chicago: University of Chicago Press, 1986.

Madison, Gary. "Did Merleau-Ponty Have a Theory of Perception?" In *Merleau-Ponty, Hermeneutics, and Postmodernism,* ed. Thomas W. Busch and Shaun Gallagher, 83–106. Albany: State University of New York Press, 1992.

———. *The Hermeneutics of Postmodernity.* Bloomington: Indiana University Press, 1988.

O'Neill, John. *The Communicative Body.* Evanston, Ill.: Northwestern University Press, 1989.

Schmidt, James. *Maurice Merleau-Ponty: Between Phenomenology and Structuralism.* London: Macmillan, 1985.

Sullivan, Shannon. "Domination and Dialogue in Merleau-Ponty's *Phenomenology of Perception.*" *Hypatia* 12 (Winter 1997): 1–19.

# 6

# Merleau-Ponty and Ricoeur on Perception, Finitude, and Transgression

PAUL RICOEUR once claimed that Merleau-Ponty was "the greatest of the French phenomenologists" (ND 1). On those occasions, however, when he commented at any length on Merleau-Ponty, he was severely critical. One case in point occurs in his essay "Existential Phenomenology":

> In Merleau-Ponty . . . the description of the "owned body" is entirely in the service of a philosophy of finitude or of an exorcism of standpointless thinking; ultimately it is in the service of a philosophy without an absolute. The *Phenomenology of Perception* should be followed from one end to the other without reference to the true object, seen from nowhere, which would justify the possibility of perception, even without ever denying the inherence of consciousness in a point of view. . . . One can only wonder . . . how the moment of reflection on the unreflected, how the devotion to universality and truth, and finally how the philosophical act itself are possible if man is so completely identified with his insertion into his field of perception, action, and life. (EP 209)

In the light of these remarks, it is possible to read the opening chapters, devoted to perception and finitude, of Ricoeur's *Fallible Man* as an extended critique of Merleau-Ponty, though he is not mentioned by name.

The thrust of Ricoeur's reflections on finitude is that "we must speak of infinitude as much as of human finitude" (FM 7). The experience of finitude originates with the body: "Every experience of finitude refers back this unusual relation I have with my body" (FM 29). The body's primacy in experience lies in the "percept" where there occurs a "primary appearing" of meaning which is foundational for all subsequent "secondary strata." The perspectival character of perception identifies perception as finite: "Finitude is identified with the notion of point of view or perspective" (FM 35). The perceived object has an "insurmountable and invincible property of presenting itself from a certain angle" so that the "object is never more than a presumed unity of the flux of these silhouettes" (FM 32). Correlatively, the perspectives of the object refer back to the mobile body of the perceiver. At this point Ricoeur asks: "All perception is perspectival, but how could I recognize a perspective, in the very act of perceiving, if *in some way* I did not escape from my perspective?" (FM 40). His answer invokes speech: "If I now note that to signify is to intend, the transgression of the point of view is nothing else than speech as the possibility of expression, and of expressing the point of view itself. Therefore, I am not merely a situated onlooker, but a being who intends and expresses as an intentional transgression of the situation. As soon as I speak, I speak of things in their absence and in terms of their non-perceived sides" (FM 41). Language here comes to the aid of the body: "Thus I judge of the entire thing by going beyond its given side into the thing itself. This transgression is the intention to signify. Through it I bring myself before a sense which will never be perceived anywhere by anyone, which is not a superior point of view, which is not, in fact, a point of view at all but an inversion into the universal of all points of view" (FM 41). The intention to signify (language) brings about a transcendental unity of the various perspectives, which allows the latter to be significant: "We need the 'name,' " Ricoeur writes, "to give a ground to the meaning-unity; the non-perspectival unity of the thing. . . . Language, in so far as it penetrates all the sensory appearances of the thing, causes perception to be significative" (FM 45). Given this essential relationship between signifying and perception, "the project of a phenomenology of perception, wherein the moment of saying is postponed and the reciprocity of saying and seeing destroyed, is ultimately untenable" (FM 42). Human reality is both body (perspective) and speech (word), intelligible only in terms of a dialectic of finitude/infinitude.

Ricoeur's critique goes to the heart of Merleau-Ponty's project, for it challenges the attempt, begun in *The Structure of Behavior,* to overcome the traditional discourse of understanding and sensibility that permeates Ricoeur's views in *Fallible Man*. In *The Structure of Behavior*, Merleau-Ponty defines a thing as "a concrete unity capable of entering into a multiplicity of relations without losing itself" (SB 118). The "concrete unity" was understood as a gestalt, a whole whose parts are mutually implicatory and express one another. In a thing, for Merleau-Ponty, the structure and material are inseparable. However, in *The Structure of Behavior* he attributed the perception of the thing to "symbolic behavior," invoking intellectualist terminology. In the *Phenomenology of Perception* he clearly attributes the perception of things to perception, and perception to the body: "I perceive with my body" (PP 326). The thing as a perceptual significance—for example, the ash tray—is not "a certain idea of the ash tray which co-ordinates its sensory aspects. . . . [T]he perceived thing is not an ideal unity" (PP 16). The linkage, merging, reference, expression of one aspect of a thing to another is a "transitional synthesis," a sensible logic that the body comes to understand through a practical dealing with things.

Recall Ricoeur's position: "I anticipate the thing itself by relating the side that I see to those that I do not see but which I *know*. Thus I judge of the entire thing by going beyond its given side into the thing itself. This is the intention to signify" (FM 41). Ricoeur's sense of "know" here is, in terms of Merleau-Ponty's position, intellectualistic, since, for Ricoeur, sensibility is impoverished to the point of standing in need of support by the understanding. The understanding supplies the meaning of "thing" for a perception unable to surpass imprisonment in perspective. For Merleau-Ponty, the "thing" as transcending perspective, whereby unseen sides are grasped as co-present, is understood by the body:

> I grasp the unseen side as present, and I do not affirm that the back of the lamp exists in the same sense that I say the solution of a problem exists. The hidden side is present in its own way. . . . It is not through an intellectual synthesis which would freely posit the total object that I am led from what is given to what is not actually given; that I am given, together with the visible sides of the object, the nonvisible ones as well. It is, rather, a kind of practical synthesis; I can touch the lamp, and not only the side turned toward me, but also the other side; I have only to extend my hand to hold it. (PrP 14)

There is evident in perception a paradox of immanence and transcendence: "immanence, because the perceived object cannot be foreign to him who perceives; transcendence, because it always contains something more than what is actually given" (PP 16). The body deals with these things with a certain familiarity and catches on to the "style" or way it is with things, which are the correlates of the perceiving body as an "I can," a mobile system of virtual powers. Thus the "style" of perceptual things as indwelled by the body is such that the body "understands" the invisible side of things as co-present with the visible "in its own way." In this way, there is no need to interject ideality or judgment into perception to constitute the thing as a thing.

The transgression from perspective to thing was only one aspect of Ricoeur's charge against a philosophy of finitude. Far more damaging in Ricoeur's estimation is the threat to a philosophy of finitude of being trapped in the singularity of the lived perspective, unable to achieve "universality and truth" or even allow for the possibility of "the philosophical act itself." In fact, Merleau-Ponty, in the well-known preface to *Phenomenology of Perception,* himself raises this issue when he recognizes that "our existence is too tightly held in the world to be able to know itself as such at the moment of its involvement," and that "it requires the field of ideality in order to become acquainted with and to prevail over facticity" (PP xv). For this reason, and especially in the light of Ricoeur's criticism, his claim later in this work that there is no such thing as "the purely lived-through" must be underlined: "It is true that we should never talk about anything if we were limited to talking about those experiences with which we coincide, since speech is already separation. Moreover, there is no experience without speech, as the purely lived-through has no part in the discursive life of man" (PP 337). One could say that the chapter "The Body as Expression, and Speech" forms the crucial argument of *Phenomenology of Perception* against modern dualisms of mind/body, understanding/sensibility, reason/fact, interior life/external manifestation, with his contention that "inner life is an inner language" (183 PP). Since "thought is no 'internal thing' " and "thought and expression are simultaneously constituted" (PP 183), the solitary self gives way to the social and communicative self. Merleau-Ponty insists, however, that the interweaving of

words and perception in no way frees one from point of view—
or, as Ricoeur suggests, in any way releases one from finitude.
Language may tempt in this direction, and is in this way dangerous. Very much in the spirit of Nietzsche, Merleau-Ponty attempts to unmask entrenched convictions about timeless and
absolute truth. He insists that meaning is inseparable from its expression and that this is clear in art. In dance, for example, the
meaning is inseparable from bodily movement. Speech, for him,
is in no way different, since the meaning resides in the words:
"An idea is necessarily linked to an act of expression, and owes to
it its appearance of autonomy. It is a cultural object, like the
church, the street, the pencil or the Ninth Symphony" (PP 390).
If the "content" of an expression has no existence freed from the
expression, the life of ideas is a life of repetition or tradition. "The
non-temporal is the acquired":

> To give expression is not to substitute, for new thought, a system
> of stable signs to which unchangeable thoughts are linked, it is to
> ensure, by the use of words already used, that the new intention
> carries on the heritage of the past, it is at a stroke to incorporate the
> past into the present, and weld that present to a future, to open a
> whole temporal cycle in which the "acquired" thought will remain
> present as a dimension, without our needing henceforth to sum-
> mon it up or reproduce it. (PP 392)

Merleau-Ponty does not at all deny "the universal" or "truth,"
but is attempting to rethink them in terms of finitude, as Ricoeur
defends them in terms of their modern formulations. Language
and speech do not of themselves bring about the universal, for
Merleau-Ponty, but in giving expression to point of view they
allow for exchange with other points of view. What transgresses
or exceeds *my* point of view is the point of view of the *Other*.
Dialogue, in which one comes to recognize a difference of perspectives, establishes the awareness of the limitations of point of
view, the possibility of critique, and the goal of (universal) agreement across points of view. In the chapter "Other People and the
Human World," Merleau-Ponty adverts to "the experience of
dialogue," which is described as a "shared operation of which
neither of us is the creator," where the Other and I "co-exist
through a common world," where "the objection which my in-

terlocutor raises to what I say draws from me thoughts which I had no idea I possessed, so that at the same time that I lend him thoughts, he reciprocates by making me think too" (PP 354). He offers an interesting example of dialogue and the creation of mutual understanding in the chapter "The Thing and the Natural World" when he discusses communication with a hallucinator:

> There is no privileged self-knowledge, and other people are no more closed systems than I am myself. . . . I misunderstand another person because I see him from my point of view, but then I hear him expostulate, and finally come round to the idea of the other person as a center of perspectives. Within my own situation that of the patient whom I am questioning makes its appearance and, in this bipolar phenomenon, I learn to know both myself and others. . . . I am sitting before my subject and chatting with him; he is trying to describe to me what he "sees" and what he "hears"; it is not a question of taking him at his word, or of sticking to my point of view, but of making explicit my experience as it is conveyed to me in my own, and his hallucinatory belief and my real belief, and to understand one through the other. (PP 338)

Reality circulates, breaking free of confinement to perspective, in communication. The Other makes an appearance "within my own situation" without being reduced to the terms of that situation. As a "bipolar" phenomenon, dialogue, through a communicative exchange, gropes toward mutual understanding.

Ricoeur was right to characterize *The Phenomenology of Perception* as "a philosophy of finitude . . . an exorcism of standpointless thinking." It is questionable, however, whether he grasped the radicality of that philosophy, which would reject the very categories he used to announce its deficiency. As mentioned, it is not an issue of Merleau-Ponty's rejection of universality, truth, and philosophy, but rather of an effort to reunderstand them within a philosophy of finitude. Merleau-Ponty is clear about this in his later work:

> Since we are all hemmed in by history, it is up to us to understand that whatever truth we may have is to be gotten not in spite of but through our historical inherence. Superficially considered, our inherence destroys all truth; considered radically, it founds a new idea of truth. As long as I cling to the ideal of an absolute spectator, of knowledge with no point of view, I can see my situation as

nothing but a source of error. But if I have once recognized that through it I am grafted onto every action and all knowledge which can have a meaning for me, and that step by step it contains everything which can *exist* for me, then my contact with the social in the finitude of my situation is revealed to me as the point of origin of all truth. (S 109)

In something of a defense of Ricoeur's reading of *Phenomenology of Perception,* it must be admitted that the social/communicative transgression of perspective remains peripheral to the main thesis, that of the "primacy of perception." While insisting that ideality and perception are interwoven, Merleau-Ponty throughout *Phenomenology of Perception* equally insists that within the ideality/perceptual nexus lies a foundation of ideality upon perception. In one sense, the full sense, of perception, there is an "ambiguous" mix of motility, sexuality, language, past experience. In another, narrower sense of perception—what Merleau-Ponty calls "natural perception"—he speaks of a sensible perception subtending, and apparently isolable from, these other elements of the mix: "We are trying to describe the *phenomenon* of the world, that is, its birth for us in that field into which each perception sets us back, where we are as yet still alone, where other people will appear only at a later stage, in which knowledge and particularly science have not so far ironed out and levelled down the individual perspective. It is through this birth that we are destined to graduate to a world, and we must therefore describe it" (PP 256). Here the social is deferred, as well as knowledge, and even a world, yet the very *description* of this "individual perspective" would depend on the very social elements it wants to defer. There is, then, a tension in *Phenomenology of Perception* forming around texts which express the fuller, ambiguous sense of perception and the narrower sense of a "natural perception." When push comes to shove, I believe that the narrower sense of perception must give way to ambiguity. Here I find myself in total agreement with Gary Madison when he writes, in regard to the notion of a "natural perception": "What traditionally has been referred to as 'perception' no longer figures in Merleau-Ponty's postfoundationalist mode of thinking."[1] The fuller sense of perception undercuts the traditional separation between sensibility and ideality and opens to the notion of dialogical universality.

While the role of social transgression of perspective remains undeveloped in *Phenomenology of Perception,* it becomes thematic and a central concern in Merleau-Ponty's subsequent writings. For example, "The Child's Relations with Others" attempts to fuse corporeal and social conditions. Merleau-Ponty tells us that "in reality the two orders are not distinct; they are part and parcel of a single global phenomenon" (PrP 108). The child's sense of self is seen to develop through stages of various social and linguistic relationships, embedding it in the dimension of communicative rationality and universality. The child, Merleau-Ponty tells us, will use the word "I" when "he has become conscious of his own proper perspective, distinct from those others, and when he has distinguished all perspectives from the external object. . . . The *I* arises when the child understands that every *you* that is addressed to him is for him an *I;* that is, that there must be a consciousness of the reciprocity of points of view in order that the word *I* may be used" (PrP 150). The essays comprising *Signs* feature the communicative life, with full recognition of the saturation of perception by culture: "Through the action of culture, I take up my dwelling in lives that are not mine. I confront them and make one known to the other, I make them equally possible in an order of truth, I make myself responsible for all of them and I create a universal life" (S 75). The perspectivism of embodiment is not transgressed vertically, risen above or gotten out of, but laterally, by "a sort of *lateral universal* which we acquire through ethnological experience and its incessant testing of the self through the other person and the other person through the self" (S 120). The opening of perspective into communication creates a public life: "A language which gives our perspectives on things and cuts our relief in them opens up a further investigation" (S 77). Participation in this life draws one to "brotherhood," in the form of address and response. Embodiment and perspectivism become "incorporation" with this participation with others in communicative life. While the dissemination of being in perspectives appears to universalize or gather in the dialogue of communicative life, Merleau-Ponty constantly warns us to recognize the fundamental ambiguity and plurivocity of meaning lest one succumb to "reduction or rash transposition." His is not a communicative life based on the "same" meanings, but an interpretative life which admits of irreducible differences.

Meanwhile, Ricoeur's thought was itself taking a hermeneutic turn, beginning with *The Symbolism of Evil* (1960) and followed by *Freud and Philosophy: An Essay on Interpretation* (1965) and *The Conflict of Interpretations: Essays on Hermeneutics* (1969). His initial interest in hermeneutics came about when, in pursuing his phenomenology of the will, he encountered the indirect language of the "servile will." His growing interest in the symbol and language led him to reconsider his relationship with phenomenology. Hermeneutics supplied a remedy for the idealist elements of phenomenology that Ricoeur always criticized. Hermeneutics' commitment to "belongingness" repudiated phenomenology's foundationalism. In place of intuition, hermeneutics offered interpretation, which affected the subject's grasp of both the object and itself. Ricoeur's notion of the subject "understanding itself in front of the text" countered the autonomous drift of the *cogito* in phenomenology. His attention shifted from Husserl and the problems surrounding the phenomenological method to thinkers such as Heidegger, Gadamer, and Habermas and to a new set of problems involved in their discourses. Ricoeur's distinctive voice could clearly be heard in his dialogue with these people in his views on metaphor, narrative identity, psychoanalysis, and the role of the critical social sciences. As a result of his turn to hermeneutics, no longer would Ricoeur allude to language as a "view from nowhere," in contrast with the perspectivism of perception. The very antinomy of finitude/infinitude would be displaced by a new one, that of belonging/distantiation.

Ricoeur's sensitivity to the finite was phenomenologically represented by his commitment to Marcel's discourse on embodiment. His sensitivity to the finite was hermeneutically represented by Heidegger (and Gadamer), where language itself was understood to be radically finite, embedded within a form of life. Heidegger's "being-in-the-world" represents the sense of "belongingness" which characterizes all finite existence. Ricoeur is bothered, however, by what he perceives to be the over-restrictiveness of Heidegger's understanding of belongingness. In a question that, in a different register, echoes the question he put to the *Phenomenology of Perception,* which he suspected of locking one into perspective too closely, Ricoeur asks of Heidegger: "How is it possible to introduce a critical instance into a consciousness of belonging which is expressly defined by the rejection of distantiation?" (TH 61). It is a question once again of transgression, this time the transgression of one's "horizon," or sense of self, others, world, time, value, and so forth—in other words, one's lifeworld. It is not a matter of leaving point of view, but rather of thinking transgression within point of view. Ricoeur turns to Gadamer, for "according to Gadamer, if the finite condition of historical knowledge excludes any overview, any final synthesis in the Hegelian manner, nevertheless this finitude does not enclose me in one point of view. Wherever there is a situation, there is an horizon which can be contracted or enlarged" (TH 61–62). Insofar as a situation is imbued with signs, language (and therefore analogous to a text), it is not fixed, but open to interpretation and to change.

Ricoeur emphasizes, more than Gadamer, the instability and contingency that affect communicative life, whether it be a case of conducting an ordinary conversation, reading a poem, or translating from across lifeworlds. While borrowing at times Gadamer's discourse of a "fusion of horizons" to mark the "intersection" of points of view, Ricoeur reminds us that "the fusion of horizons excludes the idea of a total and unique knowledge [and] implies a tension between what is one's own and what is alien, between the near and the far; and hence the play of difference is included in the process of convergence" (TH 62). To emphasize the impossibility of coincidence, Ricoeur highlights the role of distantiation in his hermeneutics. For nineteenth-century Romantic hermeneutics, distantiation was equivalent to alienation, and hermeneutic method, as a method of reentering the past, constituted its cure. For Ricoeur, however, distantiation is "productive" of meaning: "The main implication of this for hermeneutics would concern the new specific kinds of *distantiation* linked to the production of discourse as a work. A poem is a good example. But a narrative would serve the same purpose. A work of discourse, as a work of art, is an autonomous object at a distance from the authorial intention, from its initial situation . . . and from its primitive audience. For this very reason it is open to an infinite range of interpretations" (RL 75). In the case of discourse as a work, the work, distanced from authorial intention, is given reference by its readers, who must render the work meaningful on the basis of the tension between their own horizons of meaning and the structure of the work itself.

When Ricoeur, in taking the hermeneutic turn, abandoned his earlier Kantian/Husserlian phenomenology, and when Merleau-Ponty went on to develop the more expansive and ambiguous version of perception (as opposed to "natural" perception), the basis of their earlier differences over perception/transgression gave way and common ground formed around investigations of communicative life. This is evident in Merleau-Ponty's notion of the "lateral universal" and Ricoeur's understanding of the "fusion of horizons." In his late works "Eye and Mind" and *The Visible and the Invisible,* Merleau-Ponty, in the eyes of many critics, appears to abandon his commitment to the communicative life in favor of cultivating his own philosophical garden. "Quietism" and "narcissism," say Sartre[2] and Lefort[3] of the late work. How, if at all, did his late work bear upon finitude, transgression of perspective, the communicative life, and, in general, the issues that have defined the Merleau-Ponty/Ricoeur connection?

The later works convincingly put to rest the nostalgia for origins, for a recovery of a primitive level of experience, which some critics believe haunts *Phenomenology of Perception.* "A lost immediate, arduous to restore, will, if we do restore it, bear within itself the sediment of critical procedures through which we will have found it anew; it will therefore not be the immediate" (VI 72). The ontology of *The Visible and the Invisible* is an ontology of hermeneutic experience, rejecting the notions of coincidence and fusion with things or the past:

> And likewise there is no coinciding with the being of the past: if the pure memory is the former present preserved, and if, in the act of recalling, I really become again what I was, it becomes impossible to see how it could open to me the dimension of the past. And if in being inscribed within me each present loses its flesh, if the pure memory into which it is changed is an invisible, then there is indeed a past, but no coinciding with it—I am separated from it by the whole thickness of my present; it is mine only by finding in some way a place in my present, in making itself present anew. (VI 122)

A derivative of this hermeneutical ontology is his view of ideality as the invisible of the visible, precluding something like a purely "natural perception," for the invisible is "directly in the infrastructure of vision" (VI 145). Universality appears in the "hinges" and "dimensions" of perceptual experience. Pure nominalism is denied along with the pure ideal or universal in favor of the "flesh," whose "primordial property" is of "being an individual, of being also a dimension and a universal" (VI 142). One experiences in terms of multiple and overlapping dimensions, such as color, sound, the past, and language, which are levels "in terms of which every other experience will henceforth be situated" (VI 151). The universality of these levels or "hinges" of experience is implicit and insufficient to thematize one's perspective as a perspective. For this, Others are necessary: "Visions other than our own . . . bring out the limits of our factual vision, they betray the solipsist illusion that consists in thinking that every going beyond is a surpassing accomplished by oneself. For the first time I appear to myself completely turned inside out" (VI 145). A plurality of perspectives exists within the weave of the dimensions of Being: "We are moments of the same syntax . . . we belong to the same Being" (VI 83).

The linkage of "syntax" and "Being" marks perhaps the distinctive contribution of *The Visible and the Invisible*. It marks Merleau-Ponty's appropriation of the diacritical, oppositional, relative elements of structural linguistics to establish a sense of difference, transcendence, transgression which goes beyond *Phenomenology of Perception*. The weave of the dimensions of Being in flesh incorporates difference in the sense of diacritical opposition. Being's "way" is flesh as an overlapping of dimensions that constitutes a meaningful identity in opposition with each other. It is this appropriation, albeit highly idiosyncratic, that, I believe, separates the hermeneutics of Merleau-Ponty and Ricoeur. Their hermeneutics is occasioned by a fundamental "lack of coincidence" in experience, but each understands this lack of coincidence differently. Lack of coincidence, for Ricoeur, is *distantiation,* which he tells us is "a fundamental characteristic of the very historicity of human experience, namely, that it is communication in and through distance" (HFD 131). Distance is linked to objectification: "Interpretation is the reply to the fundamental distantiation constituted by the objectification of man in the works of discourse, and objectification comparable to that expressed in the products of his labor and his art" (HFD 33). Ricoeur's discourse shows the influence of Hegel in this regard, despite the fact that he is clear about his rejection of Hegel's absolute knowledge and in favor of the open-endedness of interpretation.[4] Merleau-Ponty's hermeneutics is based on a sense of distance he calls *écart:*

> It is therefore necessary that the deflection (*écart*) without which the experience of the thing or the past would fall to zero, be also openness upon the thing itself, to the past itself, that it enter into their definition. What is given, then, is not the naked thing, the past itself such as it was in its own time, but rather the thing ready to be seen, pregnant—in principle as well as in fact—with all the visions one can have of it, the past such as it was one day *plus* an inexplicable alteration, a strange distance—bound in principle as well as in fact to a recalling that spans that distance but does not nullify it. What there is is not a coinciding by principle or a presumptive coinciding and a factual non-coinciding, a bad or abortive truth, but a privative non-coinciding, a coinciding from afar, a divergence, and something like a "good error." (VI 124–25)

Meaningful experience itself depends upon a "deflection," a difference. Non-coincidence is not an alienation, but a condition for meaning and the appearance of anything at all. The body and language are not, he tells us, "screens" over Being, preventing us from grasping the real goods, but are the differences which are productive of meaningful experience. In fact, body and language are not transcendental or anthropocentric conditions foisted upon being, but rather the very differentiations of experienced being itself, its own conditions of appearance, its own "syntax." Ricoeur's "objectification" and Merleau-Ponty's "strange distance" are quite different. To protect the existential, communicative use of language, Ricoeur distanced it from structuralism by differentiating the latter as *la langue* and the former as *la parole*. Each has its own "logic," as it were. The diacritical opposition of linguistic elements has its place in *la langue*, not in *la parole*, which functions hermeneutically in terms of communicative subjectivities, subject matter, reference, historicity. "What is absolutely important to me," writes Ricoeur, "is the recognition of the discursive order as being settled by no discussion concerning the semiological order and as calling for its own analysis."[5] Merleau-Ponty, however, came to see the logic of Saussurean linguistics as "characteristic of Being," and as woven into experience in all its dimensions. Distance, differentiation, is not the product of objectification, but the condition of finitude, of all meaningful experience: "If coincidence is lost, this is no accident; if Being is hidden, this is itself a characteristic of Being" (VI 122). As opposed to the temporal distantiation of Ricoeur, Merleau-Ponty's *écart* admits of both temporal and spacial differentiation: "Transcendence is identity within difference" (VI 225). All positivity is shot through with difference. Individual beings are formed by "segregation." "Distance," he tells us, "is not the contrary of . . . proximity, it is deeply consonant with it" (VI 135). Time itself, for Merleau-Ponty, belongs to Being, to flesh, as the weave, with other dimensions of experience, of difference and gathering.

With respect to this appropriation of structuralism to account for differences, Merleau-Ponty is closer to Derrida than to Ricoeur. Merleau-Ponty's claim that "if coincidence is lost, this is no accident; if Being is hidden, this is itself a characteristic of Being" echoes, in a significant way, Derrida's insistence that "if totalization has no meaning, it is not because the infinity of a field cannot be covered by a finite glance or a finite discourse, but because the nature of the field—that is, language and a finite language—excludes totalization."[6] On the questions of lack of coincidence, criticism of philosophies of "presence," and nostalgia for primitive origins, I find agreement between Merleau-Ponty and Derrida. However, Merleau-Ponty's notion of spacing in *écart* belongs to a discourse of Being and dialectics of expression, whereas Derrida's notion of spacing as "abyss" places it on a level prior to expression and meaning. Indeed, Derrida reaches *différance* through a grammatological reduction of meaning, whereas Merleau-Ponty, for whom all reduction is incomplete, finds *écart* in the tissue of experience itself. Flesh is tissue, pulp, with the denotation of a fibrous unity. *Différance* produces meaning for Derrida and of itself disseminates meaning in free play. Unity in the form of "totalization" is a ruse of metaphysics to stem the free play of meanings. Perhaps it is Derrida who best articulates what I believe his principal disagreement with Merleau-Ponty might be over difference, when he responds to an interviewer's question about dissemination, exhibiting an evident anxiety over unity: "I distinguish in a number of places between polysemy and dissemination. Polysemy is a multiplicity of meaning, a kind of ambiguity, which nevertheless belongs to the field of sense, of meaning, of semantics, and which is determined within the horizon of a certain grouping, gathering together. . . . Dissemination is something which no longer belongs to the regime of meaning; it exceeds not only the multiplicity of meanings, but also meaning itself."[7] Language, while central to Merleau-Ponty's later thought, interweaves with, and does not reduce, the field of sensibility. Embodiment is in weave with language and is reversible with it. Embodiment is a sort of gravitational force on language so that, for Merleau-Ponty, language does not break free of sensibility in dissemination, but circulates within the levels of sensibility and embodied expression. This does not reduce language in traditional empiricist fashion, for language in its dimensions of usage continually saturates, interprets, and surpasses particular forms or sedimentations of sensible expression. The sensible haunts language, and language always feels its trace. This is, in a way, the theme of Jerry Gill's *Merleau-Ponty and Metaphor*. According to Gill, "Merleau-Ponty's view of language in general clearly entails a commitment to the primacy of the metaphoric mode in relation to every form of human linguistic activity."[8] At the heart of Merleau-Ponty's own metaphors is embodiment, for he is attempting, according to Gill, to show how embodiment is implicated in all language use:

> The image of "the flesh" is used by Merleau-Ponty to signify the commonality of human experience and form of life necessary to make shared knowledge and communication possible. Our common human embodiment serves as the "language beneath language," as the place of "intersection" or overlap between individual persons, which unites our diversity and makes a spoken language possible and necessary. In this way the metaphor of flesh also serves as an excellent image of the metaphoric mode, since it too involves the overlapping of seemingly disparate terms and phrases, thereby uniting what appears to be distinct and separate meanings.[9]

I take this to mean that there is no univocally common notion of embodiment that serves to unite apparent diversity, but that embodiment and sensibility, as always existing in diversely elaborated forms or constellations (not essences, but "tufts" and "thickets" of meaning), are never incommensurable, being always incarnated forms, and as such always exhibiting metaphorical unity. Metaphor is not, for Merleau-Ponty, the disseminative effect of a grammatological spacing, but rather itself the way of Being, which can only be found circulating in the life of incarnate communicators. Being is incorporated not in a metaphysical totality, but in an open-ended and always productive communicative life.

One of Merleau-Ponty's final pronouncements was that "reversibility . . . is the ultimate truth" (VI 155). It is reversibility that enables and calls for the circulation of Being. Reversibility is, for Merleau-Ponty, a phenomenon of embodiment which pivots on difference, upon *écart,* the non-coincidence of the touching/touched. But that very non-coincidence ("that difference without contradiction") is what permits the circulation of the touching and the touched. One's body circulates upon itself in its various sensible dimensions, with the bodies of Others:

> There is a circle of the touched and the touching, the touched takes hold of the touching; there is a circle of the visible and the seeing, the seeing is not without visible existence; there is even an inscription of the touching in the visible, of the seeing in the tangible—and the converse; there is finally a propagation of these exchanges to all the bodies of the same type and of the same style which I see and touch—and this by virtue of the sensible which, laterally, makes the organs of my body communicate and founds the transitivity from one body to another. (VI 143)

In addition, "the reversibility that defines flesh exists in other fields" (VI 144), as, for example, sensible dimensions interweave with language so that the latter appears "directly in the infrastructure" of the sensible, while the sensible, sublimated in the flesh of language, signifies open-endedly and metaphorically.

If reversibility is the centerpiece of his ontological thinking, I must emphatically disagree with critics such as Sartre and Lefort who see in the later Merleau-Ponty a soul disillusioned with politics and the communal life, who retreats for solace into quietism and narcissistic reverie. Rather, I see Merleau-Ponty developing an ontology of the circulation of Being, an ontology befitting his insights into the incorporation of embodied perspectives by means of a dialogical, communicative life.

## WORKS OF MERLEAU-PONTY CITED

PP    *Phenomenology of Perception.* Trans. Colin Smith. New York: Humanities Press, 1962 (*Phénoménologie de la perception.* Paris: Gallimard, 1945).

PrP   *The Primacy of Perception and Other Essays.* Ed. James Edie. Evanston, Ill.: Northwestern University Press, 1964 (contains the cited essays "The Primacy of Perception" and "The Child's Relations with Others").

S     "The Philosopher and Sociology." In *Signs,* trans. Richard McCleary, 98–113. Evanston, Ill.: Northwestern University Press, 1964 (*Signes.* Paris: Gallimard, 1960).

SB    *The Structure of Behavior.* Trans. Alden Fisher. Boston: Beacon Press, 1963 (*La Structure du comportement.* Paris: Presses Universitaire de France, 1942).

VI    *The Visible and the Invisible.* Trans. Alphonso Lingis. Evanston, Ill.: Northwestern University Press, 1968 (*Le Visible et l'invisible.* Paris: Gallimard, 1964).

## WORKS OF RICOEUR CITED

EP    "Existential Phenomenology." In *Husserl: An Analysis of His Phenomenology,* trans. Edward G. Ballard and Lester E. Embree, 202–12. Evanston, Ill.: Northwestern University Press, 1967.

FM    *Fallible Man.* Trans. Charles Kelbley. Chicago: Regnery, 1965 (*L'homme faillible.* Paris: Aubier, 1960).

HFD   "The Hermeneutic Function of Distantiation." In *Hermeneutics and the Social Sciences,* ed. and trans. John Thompson, 131–44. Cambridge: Cambridge University Press, 1981.

ND      "New Developments in Phenomenology in France: The Phenomenology of Language." *Social Research* 34 (1967): 1–30.

TH      "The Task of Hermeneutics." In *Hermeneutics and the Human Sciences,* ed. and trans. John Thompson, 43–62. Cambridge: Cambridge University Press, 1981.

## NOTES

1. Gary Madison, "Did Merleau-Ponty Have a Theory of Perception?" in *Merleau-Ponty, Hermeneutics, and Postmodernism,* ed. Thomas W. Busch and Shaun Gallagher (Albany: State University of New York Press, 1992), 83.

2. Jean-Paul Sartre, "Merleau-Ponty," in *Situations* (New York: Fawcett, 1965), 205.

3. Claude Lefort, "Flesh and Otherness," in *Ontology and Alterity in Merleau-Ponty,* ed. Galen Johnson and Michael Smith (Evanston, Ill.: Northwestern University Press, 1990), 3–13.

4. On the level of hermeneutics, Ricoeur insists that "the conflict of interpretations is insurmountable and inescapable." "Appropriation," in *Hermeneutics and the Human Sciences,* ed. and trans. John Thompson (Cambridge: Cambridge University Press, 1981), 193. However, it is becoming increasingly clear that Ricoeur is pursuing, beyond the practice of hermeneutics, a "speculative discourse that orders the final concepts structuring the discourse employed in a hermeneutic philosophy, as they structure, in each instance in a different manner, every philosophical discourse concerned with hierarchizing its levels of conceptuality." "Reply to Gary Madison," in *The Philosophy of Paul Ricoeur,* ed. Lewis Hahn (LaSalle, Ill.: Open Court, 1995), 94. For this reason, Ricoeur resists Madison's characterization of him as a "postmetaphysical" thinker. It remains to be seen what Ricoeur's speculative level of philosophy will look like in detail. While Merleau-Ponty's ontology employs terms such as "levels" and "dimensions" of Being, these phenomena remain doxic, their meaning restricted to their function, and their functioning open-ended, so that it would be impossible to escape their ambiguity in favor of defining them in terms of traditional categories of meaning.

5. "Philosophy and Communication: Round-table Discussion between Ricoeur and Derrida," in *Imagination and Chance: The Difference*

*between the Thought of Derrida and Ricoeur,* by Leonard Lawlor (Albany: State University of New York Press, 1992), 139.

6. Jacques Derrida, "Structure, Sign, and Play in the Discourses of the Human Sciences," in *Writing and Difference,* trans. Alan Bass (Chicago: University of Chicago Press, 1978), 289.

7. Jacques Derrida, in *French Philosophers in Conversation,* ed. Raoul Morley (New York: Routledge, 1991), 97–98.

8. Jerry Gill, *Merleau-Ponty and Metaphor* (Atlantic Highlands, N.J.: Humanities Press, 1991), 123.

9. Ibid., 142.

## WORKS CONSULTED

Caputo, John D. *Radical Hermeneutics.* Bloomington: Indiana University Press, 1987.

Derrida, Jacques. "Structure, Sign, and Play in the Discourse of the Human Sciences." In *Writing and Difference,* trans. Alan Bass, 278–93. Chicago: University of Chicago Press, 1978.

Dillon, M. C. *Merleau-Ponty's Ontology.* Bloomington: Indiana University Press, 1988.

Gill, Jerry. *Merleau-Ponty and Metaphor.* Atlantic Highlands, N.J.: Humanities Press, 1991.

Madison, Gary. "Did Merleau-Ponty Have a Theory of Perception?" In *Merleau-Ponty, Hermeneutics and Postmodernity,* ed. Thomas W. Busch and Shaun Gallagher, 83–106. Albany: SUNY Press, 1991.

———. *The Hermeneutics of Postmodernity.* Bloomington: Indiana University Press, 1988.

Morley, Raoul. *French Philosophers in Conversation.* New York: Routledge, 1991.

# Conclusion: Consensus or Creation?

IN THEIR EARLY WORKS, Camus, Marcel, Sartre, and Merleau-Ponty were sharp and relentless critics of forms of totality in thought and practice. With the absurd, Camus depicted the incompatibility between the human mind and the universe. Marcel's existentialism made its debut with the deliberate marking of thought by time and place in the *Metaphysical Journal*. While Sartre posed incommensurable modes of being in his ontology and translated totality into dangerous reverie, Merleau-Ponty decried "high-altitude" thinking in the name of pluralism of perspective. Their later works added to the critique of totality a commitment to interpretation over unmediated forms of givenness, a decentering of private lived experience in favor of language and communication, and a quest to think community beyond, but not reductive of, the individual and particular. Their works, overall, trace a path from passionate criticism of a modern reason inflated with pretension to certitude and assured of a license to dominate all forms of life, to a reason, now chastened by respect for finitude and, as inherently communicative, inextricably ethical.

To characterize, as I have (and as late existentialism does not), this reconstruction as communicative ethics and rationality runs the risk of identifying it with Habermas's project, which, with its emphasis upon the formal rules of discourse as such, is much closer to modernity than to late existentialism. The developing views of ethics and rationality in the works of Camus, Marcel, Sartre, and Merleau-Ponty are truly communicative, but differ considerably from those of Habermas. Late existentialism's ethics takes form around a view of language as protest and claim (Camus), invocation (Marcel), address (Sartre), and call (Merleau-Ponty), in which the Other appears, beyond objectification (even in terms of rules), in recognition and respect, marking their views closer to Levinas than to Habermas. That they all chose art as their paradigm of the communicative act also distinguishes their project from that of Habermas, since art, for them, evinces features antithetical to views that seek a universal consensus in terms of objective rules or a *telos* of undistorted communication or around a shared sameness of meaning. Art, for late existentialism, reveals the coming into elaboration of experience in a production or interpretive reproduction which is a mix of personal experience and imagination, of historical and cultural traditions and institutions. Elaborated experience in art (and language) is a call, an invitation, which, in soliciting response, recognizes its own incompletion and suspends closure of its meaning. Art (and language) opens, as communication, to the universal, but can never reach it because interpretation involves differences of the mix of personal experience and imagination, of historical and cultural traditions and institutions. This is why late existentialism looks for forms of an open democracy which, while valuing inclusiveness, is always negotiating its own identity.

In a related, dialogical, way, late existentialism approaches critique, deeply respectful of a situatedness which precludes a strong understanding of distantiation. Favoring a dialogical process of reflexivity through encountering diverse perspectives which offer potential for transformation, late existentialism maintains an irreducible role for experience in its claim that critical and therapeutic analysis must maintain constant relation with the peculiar experience of situated participants.

In addition to this detectable, but quite unformulated, political tendency, the traditional question of the "unity" of Being is implicated in late existentialism. Because for Camus, Marcel, Sartre, and Merleau-Ponty Being is always already "broken" into elaborations, the question of the unity of Being (or any identity) is not an objective one involving pre-given structures open to some non-elaborative knowledge. Nor can there be a question of gathering, in one comprehensive and panoramic effort, all possible perspectives and elaborations. Such a totalistic project of transgressing and unifying perspective must yield to a dialogic commu-*nity* of perspectives. The unity of Being is found in the ethical (and political) circulation of Being in the call of elaborative expressions of Being, a unity of mutual recognition and respect that does not reduce, within this unity, the alterity of interlocutors.

Given these writers' own views on communication, the works of Camus, Marcel, Sartre, and Merleau-Ponty are invitations, solicitations to think together, and to inevitably transgress their own thinking. I have only tried to contribute to what those invitations might be for us, today, who have our own questions. In response, we may well ask what place the nonhuman has in the dialogical unity of Being, what becomes of the dialogical unity of Being once pervasive forms of power to clog and control the circulation of Being are admitted, what becomes of even reconstructed forms of unity and universality in the light of the fact that differences might well be deeper than late existentialism admitted. In any case, "recovering" the texts of late existentialism is not a project of coinciding with them, but rather, to borrow words from Merleau-Ponty, "to give to the past not a survival, which is the hypocritical form of forgetfulness, but a new life, which is the noble form of memory."[1]

## NOTE

1. Maurice Merleau-Ponty, *Signs,* trans. Richard McCleary (Evanston, Ill.: Northwestern University Press, 1964), 59.

# SELECTED BIBLIOGRAPHY

### ALBERT CAMUS

*Works by Camus*

*The Myth of Sisyphus and Other Essays*. Trans. Justin O'Brien. New York: Vintage Books, 1955.
*The Plague*. Trans. Stuart Gilbert. New York: Knopf, 1948.
*The Rebel*. Trans. Anthony Bower. New York: Knopf, 1954.
*Resistance, Rebellion, and Death*. Trans. Justin O'Brien. New York: Knopf, 1960.

*Works about Camus*

Isaac, Jeffrey. *Arendt, Camus, and Modern Rebellion*. New Haven, Conn.: Yale University Press, 1992.
Sprintzen, David. *Camus: A Critical Examination*. Philadelphia: Temple University Press, 1988.

### GABRIEL MARCEL

*Works by Marcel*

*Being and Having*. Trans. Katherine Farrer. New York: Harper, 1963.
*Metaphysical Journal*. Trans. Bernard Wall. Chicago: Regnery, 1952.
*The Mystery of Being*. Trans. G. S. Fraser. 2 vols. Chicago: Regnery, 1960.
*The Philosophy of Existentialism*. Trans. Manya Harari. New York: Citadel, 1964.
*Tragic Wisdom and Beyond*. Trans. Stephen Jolin and Peter McCormick. Evanston, Ill.: Northwestern University Press, 1962.

*Works about Marcel*

Cooney, William, ed. *Contributions of Gabriel Marcel to Philosophy.* Lewiston: Mellon, 1989.
O'Malley, John. *The Fellowship of Being.* The Hague: Martinus Nijhoff, 1966.


## MAURICE MERLEAU-PONTY

*Works by Merleau-Ponty*

*Adventures of the Dialectic.* Trans. Joseph Bien. Evanston, Ill.: Northwestern University Press, 1973.
*Phenomenology of Perception.* Trans. Colin Smith. New York: Humanities, 1962.
*Signs.* Trans. Richard McCleary. Evanston, Ill.: Northwestern University Press, 1964.
*The Visible and the Invisible.* Trans. Alphonso Lingis. Evanston, Ill.: Northwestern University Press, 1968.

*Works about Merleau-Ponty*

Dillon, M. C. *Merleau-Ponty's Ontology.* Bloomington: Indiana University Press, 1988.
Madison, Gary. *The Hermeneutics of Postmodernity.* Bloomington: Indiana University Press, 1988.
O'Neill, John. *The Communicative Body.* Evanston, Ill.: Northwestern University Press, 1989.
Schmidt, James. *Maurice Merleau-Ponty: Between Phenomenology and Structuralism.* London: Macmillan, 1985.


## PAUL RICOEUR

*Works by Ricoeur*

*The Conflict of Interpretations.* Evanston, Ill.: Northwestern University Press, 1974.
*Hermeneutics and the Human Sciences.* Trans. J. B. Thompson. Cambridge: Cambridge University Press, 1981.

*Oneself as Another.* Trans. Kathleen Blamey. Chicago: The University of Chicago Press, 1992.

*Works about Ricoeur*

Clark, S. H. *Paul Ricoeur.* New York: Routledge, 1990.
Jervolino, Domenico. *The Cogito and Hermeneutics: The Question of the Subject in Ricoeur.* Dordrecht, The Netherlands: Kluwer Academic Publishers, 1990.
Reagan, Charles. *Paul Ricoeur: His Life and His Work.* Chicago: The University of Chicago Press, 1996.


## JEAN-PAUL SARTRE

*Works by Sartre*

*Being and Nothingness.* Trans. Hazel Barnes. New York: Philosophical Library, 1956.
*Critique of Dialectical Reason.* Trans. Alan Sheridan-Smith. London: New Left Board, 1976.
*Life/Situations: Essays Written and Spoken.* Trans. Paul Auster and Lydia Davis. New York: Pantheon, 1977.
*Search for a Method.* Trans. Hazel Barnes. New York: Random House, 1957.

*Works about Sartre*

Anderson, Thomas. *Sartre's Two Ethics.* LaSalle, Ill.: Open Court, 1993.
Hendley, Stephen. *Reason and Relativism: A Sartrean Investigation.* Albany: State University of New York Press, 1991.

# INDEX

Caputo, John, x
Chapsal, Madaleine, 103
"Child's Relations with Others,
The" (Merleau-Ponty), 114
choice, unconditioned (Sartre), 63
City of Ends (Kant), 66–67, 70, 73
*cogito,* the, 12, 29–30, 46, 52–53,
82, 115; of Camus, 12; and
Marcel, 29–30; and Sartre's subjectivity, 52–53; subjectivity of,
46
*cogito* tradition, 44, 45, 73; and
Husserl, 45; and Sartre as
viewed by Butler, 44
cognitive totalitarianism, 91
coherence, mind's desire for, 3
*Combat* (newspaper of the Resistance), 7, 20–21
communication, 94. *See also* art,
creative expression, language,
literature, writing
community, Camus's ideas on, 11
*Conflict of Interpretations: Essays on
Hermeneutics* (Ricoeur), 115
creative expression, 38–39
*Critique of Dialectical Reason* (Sartre), 54, 77

de Beauvoir, Simone, 52
deep identity, 47, 51
*Demythologizing Heidegger* (Caputo), x
Derrida, Jacques, 15, 98, 120–21
Descartes, René, 5, 12, 29–30
desire, and the absurd, 7–8
destiny, and exigencies of life,
54–55
dialogue (Merleau-Ponty),
80–106
"Did Merleau-Ponty Have a Theory of Perception?" (Madison),
98

*différance* (Derrida), 120–21
*Discipline and Punishment* (Foucault), 43
discourse, of production vs. transformation, 43
distantiation (communication
through distance; Ricoeur),
116, 120, 128
doubt, Marcel's view of, 30
*doxa,* 2–3, 5, 8, 24, 81, 102; Camus's relation to, 2–3; Merleau-
Ponty's view of, 81
drama and narrative, Marcel's
view of, 33–35
"Drama of the Soul in Exile, The"
(Marcel), 34

*écart* (distance within Being;
Merleau-Ponty), 89–90, 94,
119–20, 122
embodiment, 40, 52–53, 121; existentialists' use of term, 52–53;
Merleau-Ponty's view of, 121
empiricism, and idealism, 28
Enlightenment, the, 23–24
Enlightenment values, 18
*Erlebnis* (subjective experience;
Merleau-Ponty), 87
*Essai sur le logos platonicien* (Parain),
64
essentialism, and Marcel, 40
estrangement, in *The Plague,* 10
ethics: Levinas's concern for,
92–93; of speech, 94–95
existentialism, phenomenological
and poststructural, 43–61
"Existential Phenomenology"
(Ricoeur), 107
"Eye and Mind" (Merleau-
Ponty), 117

"face to face" relations (Levinas),
92–93, 95